# Kemba Walker: The Inspiring Story of One of Basketball's Most Explosive Point Guards

## An Unauthorized Biography

By: Clayton Geoffreys

# Table of Contents

# Foreword

The Charlotte Hornets franchise is one of the younger organizations in the NBA. Despite this, the organization has been blessed with several memorable players including but not limited to Alonzo Mourning, Muggsy Bogues, and Glen Rice. However, there has not been a single Charlotte Hornet quite as impactful as Kemba Walker. Since entering the league in 2011, Walker was the face of the Hornets franchise, as a dynamic point guard that ranks among the top in the league. Walker had eight incredible seasons with the Hornets before wrapping up that chapter of his career and signing with the storied Boston Celtics franchise in the 2019 offseason. Thank you for purchasing *Kemba Walker: The Inspiring Story of One of Basketball's Most Explosive Point Guards*. In this unauthorized biography, we will learn Kemba Walker's incredible life story and impact on the game of basketball. Hope you enjoy and if you do, please do not forget to leave a review!

Also, check out my website at claytongeoffreys.com to join my exclusive list where I let you know about my latest books. To thank you for your purchase, you can go to my site to download a free copy of *33 Life Lessons: Success Principles, Career Advice & Habits of Successful People*. In the book, you'll learn from some of the greatest thought leaders of different industries on what it takes to become successful and how to live a great life.

Cheers,

*Clayton Geoffreys*

*Visit me at www.claytongeoffreys.com*

# Introduction

NBA eras are defined by the players and positions that dominate the landscape during those days. Centers and big men dominated the early years of the NBA with mountains such as Bill Russell, Wilt Chamberlain, and Kareem Abdul-Jabbar becoming the staple names back in the 60s and 70s. The 80s had its share of centers that dominated the league, but the highlight of those days were perimeter players such as Michael Jordan, Magic Johnson, and Larry Bird.

While the 90s also relied mostly on centers such as Shaquille O'Neal, David Robinson, and Patrick Ewing, among others, the earlier part of the new millennium saw the birth of the NBA's reliance on versatile forwards such as Dirk Nowitzki, Kevin Garnett, Tim Duncan, and LeBron James. The NBA had only a few elite guards during that era.

However, there has been a drastic change since the late 2000s up to today's modern NBA era. The league has tended towards relying mostly on point guards but not for their ability to run plays or to make passes. This was not the time when teams relied on excellent passers such as Magic Johnson, Steve Nash, and Jason Kidd to make life easier for scorers waiting in the wings. This is an era where teams relied on point guards to do nearly everything—scoring, passing, and leading.

The NBA trend of relying on point guards started when Chris Paul was leading the New Orleans Hornets in virtually every category back in the late 2000s. Then came the time when Derrick Rose and Russell Westbrook broke onto the scene to wow crowds and fellow players alike with their jaw-dropping athletic abilities and with their penchant for doing everything on the floor. Rose became the youngest MVP in league history but has since been marred by injuries. Meanwhile, Russell Westbrook has transformed into a walking triple-double machine.

Over time, the athletic scoring point guards turned into solid shooters from the outside. Kyrie Irving breaks ankles at the perimeter only to shoot jumpers over their faces. Stephen Curry, a two-time MVP, carves space outside the perimeter to shoot three-point shots in bunches. Isaiah Thomas developed from being a final pick in the draft to become an elite scoring point guard in the league mainly because of his shooting. Damian Lillard is a player that is nearly identical to Stephen Curry in terms of shooting prowess and reliance on the three-point shot.

However, the rise of point guards in the league meant that there had been stiff competition at that position. Players that would have been called elite back in the day have been overshadowed by the ankle-breakers of Kyrie Irving, the ridiculous three-point shooting of Stephen Curry, and the triple-double averages of Russell Westbrook. Not many other point guards have been getting the attention and appreciation they deserve precisely because several other players at that position are playing better or have become more popular. One such overlooked point guard is Kemba Walker.

Kemba Walker came into the NBA with plenty of expectations on his shoulders. He was part of a 2011 Draft Class that did not have much depth but had potential. Walker was one of those players that had the potential to be great in the NBA. How could he not be? Walker had had a stellar collegiate career with the University of Connecticut Huskies. He was a fantastic player in college, particularly in the final year he had with the Huskies. Walker won the NCAA title and the Most Outstanding Player award in the country's most prestigious college basketball tournament during his final season with UConn due mainly to the miracle 11-game run he had on the way to the championship.

When Kemba Walker was drafted by a rebuilding Charlotte Bobcats (now Hornets) back in 2011 after that stellar and successful college career at UConn, he was expected to be the cornerstone of a historically struggling franchise. After all, he was the best performer in the 2011 NCAA Tournament against the best collegiate players in the country.

While Kemba Walker remained a consistent and improving presence in his stint with Charlotte during his early years, many thought it was a dead-end for him and the team. The Bobcats/Hornets hardly improved under his leadership and with him being the cornerstone of a Michael Jordan-run franchise. What was worse was that Walker seemed to have peaked early in his career.

From his sophomore season until his fourth year in the NBA, Kemba Walker remained steady and one of the many good point guards in the league. However, he was only good. Nobody classified him as great or elite. His numbers and his team's performance only served to contribute to his stagnancy and status as merely a top 20 point guard in the league. Kemba Walker's stats and his efficiency remained mostly the same for three seasons until he broke out in his fifth year.

In his fifth season in the league, Kemba Walker had grown to own the leadership role and the alpha status in the Charlotte Hornets' locker room. He had developed himself to be a deadly scorer from everywhere on the floor while also working his way within the system to give his teammates enough confidence in their quest for a playoff bid. However, with the crop of elite point guards in the league, Walker had not achieved status as one of the best playmakers in the NBA.

It was only during his sixth season in the league that Kemba Walker was finally regarded as an elite player after improving leaps and bounds concerning shooting efficiency, overall performance, and team success. While all the hype and attention were on Russell Westbrook, Stephen Curry, and Kyrie Irving, among others, Kemba Walker rose to the occasion to be classified as one of the elites after several seasons of getting overlooked.

Then, as he progressed, the player once regarded as merely a slasher and a finisher turned into one of the best three-point shooting point guards in the NBA. Hard work and hundreds of hours spent shooting the ball during the offseason allowed Walker to averaged more than 25 points during his eighth season in the league. He not only turned into an elite point guard but also became one of the best players at scoring the basketball.

After that stellar season, Walker found himself in the radar of the Boston Celtics, who immediately picked him up to be their new point guard during the offseason of 2019. At the prime of his career, he was the best player the Charlotte Hornets have seen in a very long while. However, all of that was over because he had become a part of the Boston Celtics, one of the two most historic franchises in the NBA.

With numerous expectations on his shoulder, Kemba Walker embarked on his new journey to lead a great franchise to another postseason appearance and hopefully another championship banner. The pressure might be on Walker to deliver but he has always shown his ability to come up big in clutch situations. Expect the same from him in Boston.

# Chapter 1: Childhood and Early Life

Kemba Hudley Walker was born on May 8, 1990, in one of the projects in The Bronx, New York. Despite his foreign roots, Kemba was born and raised in New York. Before leaving for college, he had spent all of his life in the Big Apple. Kemba was born to parents Paul and Andrea Walker, who both lived modest and straightforward lives in an apartment in The Bronx.

Paul Walker is a native of the island of Antigua located in the Caribbean Sea. The island itself was not very big, nor was it populous. It boasts around only 80,000 people. It was mere coincidence and fate that Paul was living next door to Mary Ambrose, the mother of his wife-to-be. Paul was unusually tall compared to the other people on the island. Despite that, he was a soft-spoken giant that spent most of his time helping Mary with her chores. He helped out with gardening and the groceries without even asking for anything in return. Mary did not even have to ask the young man for help.[i]

During those days, Paul Walker also spent his days playing for one of Antigua's best basketball teams, the Ovals. He was said to have been playing like a man among boys on the island, averaging more than 35 points and going for triple-doubles most of the time. While the competition was not at the highest level in Antigua, it was still clear that basketball ran in the blood of the Walkers.

Paul later met Andre when the latter, who was raised in The Bronx, one day visited her mother, Mary, on the island. The two quickly shared a bond after learning that they had a common belief in life. Both Paul and Andrea believed in a selfless lifestyle that does not reward one in this life but only in the afterlife.[i] They connected based on this belief and relocated to New York soon after.

Growing up, Kemba Walker had that kind of a mindset instilled in him by both of his parents. Kemba and his brother Akil Nesbitt were both raised in New York. In the Big Apple, nothing is given freely. Everyone has to work hard to get what they want. Everyone has to take the initiative and go for the throat if they wished to something achieved. Generous and selfless mindsets rarely survive the harsh reality of living in New York. However, the Walker kids got by well despite that.

Because of this, Kemba Walker sometimes found himself sleeping on the couch with his brother whenever relatives and family friends came to visit. He selflessly gave up his bed for people he hardly knew and never complained about it.[i] That was how he was raised. It was a point guard's mentality that eventually was dug deep into Kemba's personality and mindset.

While Kemba Walker may have been the nicest and most selfless young boy in person, he was a different animal on the basketball court. With basketball running deep in his genetics thanks to his father's professional background in Antigua, Walker was a killer on the basketball court. Whenever he played three on three with his dad and other neighborhood father and sons in The Bronx, he was an unstoppable scoring machine, even for his age. Paul focused on getting rebounds to feed his son possessions and to improve Kemba's confidence in himself. The Walker father and son tandem seemed unstoppable at that part of their neighborhood.

Despite the Walker tandem's tough demeanor and killer personality on the court, they reverted to their selfless and giving selves as soon as the game was over. Paul treated opponents they hardly knew to refreshments after challenging games despite the fact the physicality and the trash-talking they just had moments before. While the Walker family were friendly people, basketball was where they poured in all of their negativities and turned them into energy they ran on. This kind of a lifestyle and upbringing continued even until Kemba Walker reached high school.

## Chapter 2: High School Career

Kemba Walker attended Rice High School in Harlem, New York. He immediately played junior varsity basketball in the school. However skilled and tough Walker was at that point in his career, he was still overlooked. Kemba Walker was not even a starter when he first came to Rice. He was deemed too small for a basketball player. He was not strong, nor was he the best shooter. All he brought with him were skills and toughness he learned playing in the streets of the Bronx with his father.

Come his sophomore year, Kemba Walker made the varsity year. That was when he decided to pursue basketball as a career. He was not the typical teenager that only looked to focus on basketball the moment he could walk on his own two feet. Since he was a young boy, his mother always taught him the value of a good education. He could play basketball until his late 30's. However, throughout the rest of his life, education is what mattered more. The only reason why Walker wanted to take basketball seriously was that he wanted to go to school for free.[ii]

Kemba Walker almost did not make it to Rice High based on his family's earnings. Paul Walker was a carpenter by profession. Meanwhile, Andrea worked as a caregiver. They were a modest family earning a wage enough for them to live comfortable lives. The demands of education often proved too much for them. Kemba Walker made it to Rice on a sponsorship program. His folks only had to shell out $100 a month to send him to Harlem.[iii]

It was during his days at Rice when Kemba Walker experienced organized basketball and the intense training that came with it. He and his teammates were asked to run seven flights of stairs almost every day to train their legs and improve their conditioning on the court. Back then, Kemba was already known for his quickness. He became even quicker because of the improved strength in his legs.

Considering that Kemba Walker was not a starter in his freshman year at Rice High, the young man only worked harder to get the recognition and the attention he deserved. Kemba Walker used his quickness to focus on the defensive end by deflecting passes. He was not afraid of holding his ground against the bigger players to draw charging fouls. It did not take a long time for him to finally see plays being drawn up for him by coach Moe Hicks.

Kemba Walker took what his parents taught him to his basketball years with Rice High. He was never in a hurry. Walker was patient and selfless when waiting for his turn to shine. He never pushed himself to become a starter. As his mother said, he always waited for his turn. He never complained about it. Since his sophomore year, he waited his turn at the point guard position behind a little-known Edgar Sosa. It was only during his senior year that he garnered the attention he deserved.

Kemba Walker had a stellar senior year at Rice High. Perhaps one of his best moments was when he sunk a game-winning shot against Christ the King. The team was looking for their designated shooter Chris Fouch. However, the inbounder could not get the ball to him. Walker came out to get the ball. In a matter of seconds, he seemed to have fumbled the possession after a pump fake but got himself composed enough to hit a shot that went in as he fell on the hardwood court.[iii] Never known as a shooter in high school, that was one of Walker's finest moments as a prep player.

In 20 games that season for Rice High School, Kemba Walker had grown into a leader and five-star recruit in the nation. He was ranked fifth among point guards in the entire United States. Along with that, he was 14th overall in the recruiting class of 2008. He had averaged 18.2 points, 6.4 rebounds, 5.3 assists, and 3.3 steals as a senior. While he made it to the McDonald's All-American Game that year, it was only during the game itself that he got the recognition he deserved coming into college.

Standing six feet tall, Kemba Walker was not the tallest of point guards amongst a crop of some of the nation's best young players. The defining moment of the night for him was when he finished one of the most spectacular plays of the exhibition game. Future NBA player Al-Farouq Aminu went up high for a defensive rebound. He saw that a tiny point guard was already racing up ahead the court.

Aminu quarterbacked the play by throwing a beautiful outlet pass to the streaking Kemba Walker, who took two dribbles before he was near enough to the basket to take flight. Tailing him was the bigger point guard Jrue Holiday. It did not matter because, as Holiday was on his way to try to contest the shot, Walker was already high up in the air throwing a vicious slam dunk down on his face. As soon as he finished the play and landed on his feet, he crossed his arms and formed an "X" with it to show representation for his hometown, The Bronx.[iii] Moments like those defined his high school career as he was on his way to play for the University of Connecticut Huskies for college.

# Chapter 3: College Career

## The Spitfire Freshman off the Bench

Kemba Walker entered the University of Connecticut Huskies as a standout freshman that became an integral part of a powerhouse team in the Big East. Since the Huskies were already settled with a lineup that consisted of future NBA players AJ Price, Jeff Adrien, and Hasheem Thabeet, the freshman point guard played off the bench for UConn.

Though it was technically the same as he was in high school when he had to play behind more experienced point guards, Kemba Walker played a significant role off the bench in his freshman season having averaged 8.9 points, 3.5 rebounds, and 2.9 assists. He played more than 25 minutes per game, which was more than what any freshman bench player could ever ask. He was also a member of the Big East All-Rookie Team.

Showing off his quickness and ability to get to the basket and score points in the paint despite his height,

Kemba Walker was a standout performer in his Big East debut game against Georgetown. He scored 14 points in that win. Several games later, Walker recorded a season-high of 21 points when the Huskies won against St. John's. Though he was a small point guard playing against bigger opponents, he even managed to grab 11 rebounds when the UConn Huskies lost to Syracuse in the Big East quarterfinals.

Heading into the NCAA Tournament, Kemba Walker helped his team win 31 out of 36 games as the Huskies came in as a top seed in time for March Madness. Kemba scored ten points in the opening round win of the tournament. His best outing in the tournament and for his entire freshman season was when he had 23 points in the Elite Eight win against Missouri. However, UConn ultimately fell to Michigan State in the Final Four of the tournament.

## Sophomore Season

With AJ Price moving over to play professionally in the NBA after the 2008-09 season, Kemba Walker got promoted to the starting point guard position for his sophomore season with the UConn Huskies. However, unlike his freshman year, the Huskies were struggling that season. Other than Walker, there were no other standout players on the Huskies' roster that season.

The one positive thing that the UConn Huskies could take from that season was the tremendous growth of Kemba Walker in all facets of the game. Walker had grown to become a better leader, passer, scorer, rebounder, and defender that season. He had an incredible stat line of 16 points, six assists, and five steals in their win against Colgate. A few games later, Walker had his first double-double in college after recording 15 points and ten assists in a match against Boston University. He hit the 10-assist mark three times that season.

Kemba Walker's best game that season came against the Big East favorites, Villanova. He finished that game with 29 points as he led his team to an upset win against the favored group. He had 28 points against the Louisville Cardinals a few games later. Despite such performances, Walker was unable to lead his team alone in one of the toughest conferences in the country. UConn finished with a miserable 17-16 record and were unable to qualify for the NCAA Tournament. Kemba Walker averaged 14.6 points, 4.3 rebounds, 5.1 assists, and 2.1 steals for the season.

## Junior Year, the Miracle Run

While Kemba Walker may have had a disappointing sophomore season with the Huskies, his junior year was nothing short of stellar. He had grown into a national sensation that season, especially after retooling his jumper, which was a part of his game he needed plenty of work on. Walker also realized he had to own the leadership and alpha male role in a team that was not as deep as it was a few seasons back. Kemba Walker rose to national prominence.

Kemba Walker started the season like a house on fire after scoring a massive output of 42 points on 15 out of 24 shooting in a win against Vermont. He then had 31 points in the next game to record a total of 73 markers in a span of only two games. That was not the only early-season record that Kemba Walker had. He recorded 29 points in the second half against Wichita State, totaling 31 in that game. After that, he then had 30 points in a win against Michigan State to record three consecutive outings of scoring at least 30 points. He was the first UConn player to do that since 1967. In a span of only six games, he had totaled 180 points, which is a UConn Huskies record.

Through the first 12 games of the season, the 6-foot guard from UConn was leading the nation in scoring with over 26 points per game. BYU's Jimmer Fredette later overtook him in that regard because of his phenomenal shooting. Nevertheless, Kemba Walker continued being a one-man wrecking machine for the Huskies despite his lack of size.

Other than being one of the best scorers in the entire nation, Kemba Walker also showed qualities of a cold-blooded clutch killer. He broke the hearts of Texas fans when he sank a game-winner in the overtime period. Walker had 22 points and nine rebounds that game. He then drained a game-winning shot with only two seconds remaining against Villanova. He totaled 24 points that night. In the Big East Tournament Quarterfinals, he hit a jumper at the buzzer to give UConn the win over Pittsburgh. The Huskies eventually won the conference championship. Walker scored a record 130 points in the five games he played on his way to the Big East title. What was more improbable was that he and the team had to play all five games of the tournament for five consecutive days. After all the fatigue, they were not expected to win the title, but they did.

Kemba Walker's dream run did not end with a Big East title. Coming in leading the three-seeded UConn Huskies into March Madness, Walker dished out 12 assists on his way to securing a victory for his team in the Round of 64 in a blowout win against Bucknell. While Kemba Walker had focused more on playmaking in the first round, it was a different story against Cincinnati in the second round. Walker showed plenty of late-game heroics by going for 16 points in the final ten minutes of the match. He had 33 points to secure a Sweet 16 berth for the UConn Huskies.

Coming into the Sweet 16 matchup against San Diego State and future NBA superstar Kawhi Leonard, Kemba Walker once again showed up late in the game after the Aztecs were able to grab the lead in a tightly-contested match. Walker went on a personal run in the final nine minutes of the game. He totaled 36 points. He also made freshman Jeremy Lamb look good by making him feed off his slashes and drives to the rim. Lamb scored 24 points and missed only two baskets.

In the Elite Eight, Arizona had put all the defensive attention on the streaking point guard from The Bronx. Kemba Walker struggled to look for his shots as Arizona had put the clamps on him. He was not a one-man wrecking crew, at least for that night. Guards Jeremy Lamb and Shabazz Napier both picked up the slack to assist their leader. When the time was right, it was up to Walker to put the icing on the cake once more. He drained a step-back perimeter jumper to give the UConn Huskies an insurmountable lead with time not on Arizona's side. Kemba Walker finished the night with 20 points.

One of the toughest matchups that Kemba Walker and the UConn Huskies had to face in the NCAA Tournament was the Semi-Finals game against the Kentucky Wildcats. Featuring a deep team that had future NBA player such as point guard Brandon Knight, big man Terrence Jones, shooter Doron Lamb, and forward Darius Miller, among others, the Wildcats were the heavy favorites coming into that game.

At first, it seemed like it was going to be a game favoring the Kentucky Wildcats. The low-scoring pace slowed down the quick Kemba Walker. It was a game won on the defensive end. When it mattered most, Walker came out big again after finishing the game with a great all-around effort. He led the team to a one-point win with 18 points, six rebounds, and seven assists. After that game, Kemba Walker became a national sensation. He had led his team to an improbable 10-game winning run that had a chance to culminate with an NCAA title. No 10-game run in collegiate basketball history was arguably better than Kemba's that year.

Kemba Walker stretched and put the punctuation mark on that run with 11 consecutive wins. Nobody expected the UConn Huskies to win the national title at the end of the year. Nobody expected such a run from the small but quick guard from New York. Yet, Walker willed himself and his team to that win. He finished with 16 points in what was an ugly and fatigue-driven game. Nevertheless, the result was what mattered most. Kemba Walker ended the most incredible 11-game run in college basketball history by hoisting the NCAA championship trophy up above his head.

As the dust settled, Kemba Walker averaged 23.5 points, 5.4 rebounds, 4.5 assists, and 1.9 steals all season long. He was named First Team All-American and was one of the finalists for the College Basketball Player of the Year award. He finished second to Jimmer Fredette, who did not have a similarly successful NBA career. As the top point guard in the country, Kemba Walker was given the Bob Cousy Award. On top of all that, he was named Most Outstanding Player of both the Big East and NCAA Tournaments. Capping off his career with UConn was an inclusion in the Huskies of Honor. He was the first-ever basketball player to be given that honor.

With everything he set out to do in college already in the books, Kemba Walker was riding high on the national attention and love he was receiving because of his miracle run to the NCAA championship. He declared himself for the NBA Draft on April 12 and gave up what would have been his final season with the UConn Huskies. With the showing he had in his junior year in college, the sky was the limit for Walker when he finally got to set foot on an NBA hardwood floor.

# Chapter 4: NBA Career

## Getting Drafted

The 2011 NBA Draft Class was not the deepest one as far as talent was concerned. The class had plenty of potential amongst its younger prospects and the ones that had played overseas. Nobody was ready to become a superstar or deemed to have All-Star potential other than consensus top overall pick Kyrie Irving, who barely played an entire season for Duke in his lone freshman year.

Kyrie Irving was no doubt the top point guard in that draft class. While NBA teams were turning their attention towards the mysterious yet skilled big men that had played overseas, some were looking at the other point guards in the draft class. The NBA had seen a trend that favored point guards. The game was getting played faster. Teams were relying on the three-point shot more than they ever did before. Never has the NBA needed skilled point guards more than they did in that era.

In his lone season with Kentucky, Brandon Knight was a fantastic prospect. He could lead his team to the Final Four before losing to the UConn Huskies led by Kemba Walker, of course. Over the past few seasons, Kentucky has had the reputation of developing All-Star quality point guards. Knight had youth, talent, and skill with him coming into the draft.

Another point guard that caught plenty of attention was BYU's Jimmer Fredette. Fredette was considered the Stephen Curry of college basketball. He was pulling up and draining three-pointers far beyond the college three-point line. Walker was scoring at will despite his lack of size, speed, and athleticism. He won the College Player of the Year award after leading the nation in scoring. However, the problem was that he was not a real point guard no matter how great a shooter he was. Nevertheless, his accomplishments spoke for themselves. He was an intriguing prospect for any team.

Then, of course, there was Kemba Walker, who had the most incredible 11-game run for an overlooked team heading into the 2010-2011 college season. The way Walker led and willed that UConn Huskies team to the NCAA title was nothing short of spectacular. His miracle run spoke in itself. It was what catapulted him to getting the national attention he deserved after getting overlooked in his first two seasons. Kemba Walker showed the heart of a champion in his junior year with UConn, but did he have enough in his package to become an NBA star?

As far as physical attributes are concerned, Kemba Walker was never an impressive player. He was often considered short. Listed at 6'1", he was barely even six feet tall when he did not have his sneakers on. He was not even the biggest or strongest player since he was barely 180 pounds coming into the Draft. He did not have the widest wingspan, either. Just by looking at him, one could assess Walker's size as a liability in and of itself.

However, despite his lack of size, Kemba Walker's athletic abilities have always been top-notch. He has a maximum vertical leap of about 40 inches. His dunk on Jrue Holiday back in the 2008 McDonald's All-American classic served as a testament to how high he could get up. Walker is also described as blazingly fast. His athletic abilities were what brought him to the dance.

Offensively, Kemba Walker relies a lot on his speed and explosiveness to get buckets up on the board. He moves faster than anyone else on the floor and seemingly knows how to get to where he wants without much impediment. Despite his speed, Walker never seemed too out of control, always knowing what to do with the fast pace at which he was moving.[iv]

Despite his size, Kemba Walker was always aggressive off the dribble. He got to the basket by blowing by defenders out on the perimeter. His explosive first step put the defenders on their heels and reeling. Nobody could contain him one-on-one when he decided to take the ball to the basket off the dribble. With his speed, he was even more dangerous during transition plays.

In line with his quickness, Walker's ball-handling abilities had seen a remarkable improvement. During his junior year, he was seen splitting double teams with ease and could even change directions at full speed without losing control of himself or possession of the basketball. There was nothing he could not whenever he decided to take the basketball to the rim. He blew by his man, split double teams, eluded secondary defenders by changing direction, and attack with full aggression.

Of course, since slicing towards the basket was always his specialty, Kemba Walker knows how to attack and finish at the basket. He has an array of finishing moves at the basket to elude the bigger shot blockers. Walker can improvise his shot mid-air or re-angle his plan of attack. Whenever he is unable to elude the defenders down low, Walker is never afraid to absorb contact while finishing plays.[iv] He dives full steam ahead with all the aggression in the world to bump bodies with men double his size. Despite that, he always seems to look twice as strong as he is and can score baskets at the rim.

Whenever he is not taking his man off the dribble to attack the basket, Kemba Walker has shown a good amount of skill in creating space for himself. He knows how to make his shot fakes look convincing enough to get defenders off-balance. His speed and quickness make defenders bite quickly on his jab steps. He also eludes defenders at the perimeter by using step-backs and crossover moves. When he gets the separation he needed, he could drain jump shots from the perimeter. Most of the game-winners he hit during his final year with UConn were off shots he created for himself out in the perimeter.

As a point guard, Kemba Walker does not seem like the best playmaker in the 2011 NBA Draft Class but is a better passer than what he is often given credit for. In his four years with Rice High School, his primary focus was to get his teammates the ball. He was always a willing passer and playmaker. His first two seasons in college also showed how good of a passer he was. Walker was regarded as an underrated passer because of how good he is offensively. He knows when to get the ball to open teammates out on the wings whenever he tears defenses down with his elite-level slashing ability. Walker can thread needles to get teammates improbable good looks and can dish out bullet passes to streaking and rolling players.[iv]

Defensively, Kemba Walker has shown that he can excel on that end of the court. His lateral quickness helps him keep up with players just as fast as he is. Walker uses that ability to beat his man to the spot. Despite his short arms, he has enough speed in him to get to passing lanes or to even pressure the ball out of his man's hands.

Kemba Walker is a superb offensive player, mainly because of his speed and quickness. He has also shown potential to become a good defender. However, what made him a special player in college were not his skills, but the intangibles Walker brought with him. He never gives up on plays or games. He always gives his all out on the floor and plays with the heart of a champion. His skills in leading a team had taken a significant step, especially after the way he willed his team to an 11-game run towards the NCAA championship. What makes that even better is that he seems to enjoy the fact that his teammates look better and become more confident because of how he leads them.

Like all young prospects, Kemba Walker was not without any weakness that hindered him from becoming the consensus choice for the top overall pick. He was not even considered a top-five choice that year. Players are often evaluated more for what they lack rather than for what they could provide for a team. Kemba Walker was no different despite barely showing any weaknesses during his miracle run.

The biggest weakness that stood out is, of course, Kemba Walker's lack of size. On the offensive end, he has shown that short frame was never a hindrance. He has always made the best of the entirety of his 6-foot size by going all out on the offense. However, defense is where his lack of size becomes an issue. Walker was playing against the likes of Derrick Rose, Russell Westbrook, and John Wall, who are just as fast as he is but are a lot bigger. Bigger guards can post him down low and can even shoot over him on the perimeter. This was a red flag for any team.[v]

Kemba Walker's questionable shot selection was also a subject of criticism. Technically the lone offensive gun of UConn during his junior season, Walker nearly doubled his shot attempts from the previous season and was becoming more confident and unafraid of the big stage and big shots. However, this also led him to take shots outside his arsenal or beyond that of which he was capable. While it is not that big of a deal for him to take bad shots from time to time, it has become an issue, primarily because he is not known to be a good shooter.

On the topic of his ability to hit jump shots, Kemba Walker's Achilles heel coming into college was his lack of consistency on that part of the offense. He almost exclusively relied on his ability to get to the basket and attack the rim with reckless abandon. His jump shot was always questionable, though he has shown significant improvement over the three years he played at UConn. By the time he was a junior, he was hitting jumpers out on the perimeter, though his consistency was still lacking.

What his jumper lacked most was range. Walker barely attempted shots from the college three-point line, which is a lot shorter than the NBA arc. Despite that, he shot subpar from a distance during his stay with the Huskies. Walker's shooting stroke and form were often seen as the main suspects to why he lacked consistency and range. Kemba Walker needed to fine-tune that part of his game if he intended to produce at a high level in the NBA. He may have been able to get by well with his quickness and attacking ability, but the NBA has quicker defenders and more physical paint. It was a lot harder for Walker to rely mainly on his slashing ability if he does not develop a consistent jump shot.

Despite being heralded as a good passer, nobody expected Kemba Walker to be a point guard that dictates the offense and makes plays like a Magic

Johnson or a Steve Nash. He knows when to create looks for teammates and when to dish passes out. However, Walker's mentality is always to score the ball first. He may look like Jason Kidd for a few plays and on appropriate occasions. He will always look to put the ball in the hole before he decides to make his teammates look like All-Stars.

While Kemba Walker may have already been good at converting in the paint, he needed to develop more moves if he wanted to excel in the pro league. Walker prefers attacking the basket more than going for finesse and graceful shots like floaters and scoops. He needed to develop those kinds of shots considering he could forever absorb contact and finish over the bigger and stronger NBA paint defenders.

As draft day came, the Cleveland Cavaliers selected Kyrie Irving with the top overall pick. Forwards and big men were what comprised the rest of the lottery pick until it reached the Detroit Pistons, who were picking eighth. They plucked out the younger Brandon Knight with their draft choice, believing he could usher in a new era in Detroit. Up next were the Charlotte Bobcats.

The Bobcats, despite their ownership's legendary status in the lore of basketball, have always been one of the fodder teams in the NBA. There were years when they seemed competitive but were often one of the worst teams in the league. During the 2010-11 season, they were relying on DJ Augustin and Shaun Livingston to handle the point guard duties. That part of their roster was always considered a large hole that they needed to fill up. Michael Jordan might have thought that DJ Augustin was going to be a right starting point guard. However, that vision had not panned out, and the Bobcats needed a playmaker that could help usher the franchise towards an era where the NBA gravitated towards point guards.

Because of the team's need to get younger and better at the point position, they drafted Kemba Walker with the ninth pick of the 2011 NBA Draft.

Kemba was the third point guard chosen in that class. Kyrie Irving was the first, of course. Brandon Knight was drafted a pick ahead of him. Though Walker had a more stellar college career, both Irving and Knight were two years fresher and younger. Moreover, they were bigger point guards and had a shooting stroke that Walker was yet to develop.

Nevertheless, the guard that was often overlooked and who often played behind more experienced players was finally going to places where point guards that started over him could only dream of going. He had reached a goal only kids from The Bronx could dream to achieve. He was officially an NBA player.

## The Dreadful Rookie Season

The Charlotte Bobcats were supposed to be an improved team compared to the mediocre season they had a year before. They were 34-28 under coaches Larry Brown and Paul Silas at the end of the 2010-11 regular season. Veterans Gerald Wallace and Stephen Jackson headlined the team. With the injection of young rookies Kemba Walker and big man Bismack Biyombo, whom they traded for on the draft day, the Bobcats were expected to be more competitive.

The rookie Kemba Walker's season debut had to be pushed two months later. The NBA entered into a lockout due to a dispute between the players' union and team owners. It was only in December when a new Collective Bargaining Agreement was struck. Teams did not have too much time to prepare for the new season as training camp was shortened and rushed. This only made it more difficult for Walker to adjust to the team's system and his new teammates.

On December 26, 2011, Kemba Walker made his NBA debut in a win against the Milwaukee Bucks. In 20 minutes of play, he scored 13 points on three out of ten shooting from the field and seven out of seven from the foul line. Walker also collected seven rebounds. However, as always, he started a new basketball career by coming off the bench. He did the same at Rice High School and when he got to UConn. The NBA was no different. He played behind DJ Augustin at the point guard position.

In Walker's second game, which was a loss to the powerhouse Miami Heat, he went for 14 points while playing against the superstar trio of LeBron James, Dwyane Wade, and Chris Bosh. He made six of his nine shots in that game. However, after two good performances to start his NBA career, Walker shot blanks in his third game to score only two points. He then bounced back on a personal level against the same Miami team on January 1, 2012. He scored a new career-best of 17 points after converting six of his 13 shots. However, unlike the close game they had in their first meeting, the Bobcats lost this one by 39 points.

Five days later, Kemba Walker went for a new career-high in points. In a loss to the Atlanta Hawks, he went for 19 points on six out of ten shooting from the field. Impressively, Walker made three of his five three-pointers though he was never considered an actual threat from beyond the arc. The next time he scored an impressive outing was a week later in a loss to the Detroit Pistons. He had 16 points on a great shooting night of six out of eight from the field.

On January 14 in a game against the Golden State Warriors, Kemba Walker exploded for another career-high. He made eight of his 15 baskets, two of his four three-pointers, and five of his six free throws to record 23 points. He also added four rebounds and five assists in what was his first career start in the NBA. The Charlotte Bobcats ended up winning that game. However, the dreadful season they eventually had was only beginning. It took more than a month for them to taste victory once again.

While the Charlotte Bobcats may have been losing game after game en route to what eventually became a 16-game losing skid, Kemba Walker continued to impress as a rookie. He went over the 20-point mark a second time that season after registering 22 points in a blowout loss to the New York Knicks on January 24. He shot seven out of 17 in that game and made all six of his free throws.

On January 28, Kemba Walker impressed by registering his first career triple-double. In effect, he was also the first rookie of the class of 2011 to achieve a triple-double. He finished that loss to the Washington Wizards with 20 points, ten rebounds, and 11 assists. Interestingly enough, Walker was only the third player in Charlotte Bobcats history ever to record a triple-double. This lends proof to the idea that the Bobcats were never a very successful franchise due to a lack of good all-around players.

Walker went for at least 20 points again during that losing run. It was when he had 22 points on seven out of 16 shooting in a loss to the Phoenix Suns. Nearly a week later, Walker recorded back-to-back 20-point performances. He had 21 points in both the losses to the Philadelphia 76ers and Minnesota Timberwolves. All in all, Walker broke the 20-point barrier five times during that 16-game skid.

On February 17, Kemba Walker returned to playing bench duties after DJ Augustin returned from injury. He scored 14 points off the bench in a game where the Charlotte Bobcats finally snapped their cold spell. That was only the fourth win of the season for a team that ended up becoming one of the worst squads in league history.

The Bobcats' fifth win of the season came on March 6 against the Orlando Magic. Kemba Walker had ten points in that game after tasting the sweetness of NBA victory for only the fifth time. He had always been a winner since high school. He was just off from a historic run towards an NCAA title, but the NBA quickly brought him back down to earth. The only way for a winner to know what it truly means to win is for him to understand what it is to lose, and Walker was experiencing that first hand.

The Bobcats had their sixth win of the season on March 12 against the New Orleans Hornets. Kemba Walker finished that game with 14 points on six out of ten shooting from the field and 23 minutes off the bench. Five days later, they went for their seventh and final win of the season. It was against the Toronto Raptors. Walker did not contribute to the win. He only had two points in 12 minutes of play. From then on, the Charlotte Bobcats went for an embarrassing 23-game losing streak, which is the fifth-longest in league history.

Despite the hardship of facing loss after loss in his rookie season, Kemba Walker continued to improve his confidence as the season ended. He managed to score 20 points or more three times during that losing stretch. He even posted a double-double game against the Sacramento Kings on April 22 after going for 13 points and 11 assists. However, all of his efforts were in vain as far as salvaging that season was concerned. All he could hope for was to improve. For his team, they had to secure a highly-touted rookie in the next draft class after that awful season.

In his rookie season, the former NCAA champion and tournament Most Outstanding Player averaged 12.1 points, 3.5 rebounds, and 4.4 assists. He found that the NBA was a different monster. Walker struggled to shoot from the field against faster defenders and bigger paint protectors. He only shot 36.6% from the floor. His team was not doing so well, either. The 7-59 Charlotte Bobcats of that season ranks as the worst team in league history as far as winning percentage is concerned. No team has been worse since then.

## Getting the Start, Rise to Alpha Status

The Charlotte Bobcats continued to get younger and better after drafting Kentucky's Michael Kidd-Gilchrist with the second pick of the 2012 NBA Draft. Kidd-Gilchrist, while still offensively raw, was a ready defensive asset for the Charlotte Bobcats. However, the defense was only part of the problem for the Bobcats. They were a dreadful offensive team. It was even suggested that they should have drafted better offensive choices such as Bradley Beal or Damian Lillard. However, the franchise was confident in making Kemba Walker the team's building block. They revolved the offense around him coming into the 2012-13 season as Kemba Walker quickly rose to become not only the starting point guard but the team's alpha Bobcat and best player.

With the coaching staff's and Michael Jordan's green light, Kemba Walker made the Bobcats his team. He opened the season on November 2, 2012, scoring a new career-high of 30 points. Walker shot ten out of

21 from the field in that game. It also marked the first time he scored 30 or more points in his young NBA career. The Charlotte Bobcats, who only won seven games a season before, won that one against the Indiana Pacers.

Eight days after that career game, Walker went for another high-scoring output. He registered 26 points on ten out of 22 shooting from the field against the Dallas Mavericks to give his team their second win of the season out of five games. Walker also added six rebounds and seven assists. Yet, the most impressive part of the night was the career-best eight steals he collected that game.

After that performance, Kemba Walker then led his team to two more consecutive wins to mark the first time he has won three successive games in his NBA career. He had 17 points in a win versus the Washington Wizards on November 13 before going for 22 points, four rebounds, five assists, and four steals against the Minnesota Timberwolves. It was also during that win against the Wolves when Kemba Walker drained the first of his many game-winners. Showing the same clutch mentality and killer instinct that he displayed in college, Walker drained the go-ahead bucket to put the Bobcats up for good until the final buzzer sounded. Walker continued scoring in double digits in the first 12 games of the season. The Bobcats were 7-5 during those first 12 games. During that span, Kemba was putting up All-Star numbers of 18 points, four rebounds, six assists, and 2.3 steals.

A scoreless night against the OKC Thunder on November 16 cut Walker's double-digit scoring streak at 12. He struggled to contain Russell Westbrook that night while the triple-double machine All-Star guard contained him. Walker only played 20 minutes and could not convert a single field goal in that 45-point loss. Nevertheless, he bounced back quickly by going for another streak of consecutive double-digit scoring.

On December 5, Kemba Walker had his first double-double of the season after going for 25 points and 11 assists in a loss to the Milwaukee Bucks. He shot eight out of 15 from the floor in that narrow defeat. Unfortunately for his Bobcats, that loss was their fifth consecutive one after starting the season winning more than half of their first 12 games. What was worse was that the losing skid did not end. It seemed as if it was the 2011-12 season all over again for them.

Despite suffering loss after loss all over again, Kemba Walker kept his head up high and continued to turn in impressive performances. On December 8, he had 23 points on a 50% shooting clip in a loss to the San Antonio Spurs. Two nights later, Walker had 24 points and six assists when the Bobcats suffered a defeat at the hands of the Golden State Warriors. Five days later, he went for a new career-high for the second time that season. Kemba Walker shot 11 out of 20 from the field and hit all but one of his nine free-throw attempts to go for 32 points in a loss to the Orlando Magic. He also added seven assists in that game. He was also impressive in the match following that one as he went for 28 points, five rebounds, and seven assists in a loss to the Los Angeles Lakers.

The Charlotte Bobcats' losing streak ended at 18. It was in the final game of 2012 that they tried to forget about a bad calendar year for the team. In that win against the Chicago Bulls, Kemba Walker went for 18 points, eight rebounds, six assists, and four steals. It was a respectable performance for a guard saying goodbye to a disappointing 2012.

Kemba Walker had his first win of 2013 on January 6 against the Detroit Pistons. Reliving their Final Four encounter nearly two years ago, Walker outplayed Brandon Knight, who was drafted ahead of him in 2011. Kemba had 20 points and seven assists. Meanwhile, Knight finished with only 12 points while he was still trying to establish himself in Detroit.

On January 19, Kemba Walker registered his second double-double that season after going for 14 points and ten assists. Sadly, it came at a loss to the Sacramento Kings. That was not the only time he came up big in a loss. Two nights later, he went for a new career-high of 35 points. Walker made 12 of his 21 field goals, six of his seven three-pointers, and five of his six free throws to reach that number. However, the Bobcats tasted the bitterness of defeat at the hands of the Houston Rockets.

Kemba Walker had a near triple-double in what was a rare win for the Charlotte Bobcats. In that game against the Minnesota Timberwolves, Walker finished the game with 25 points, eight rebounds, and eight assists. He also added three steals and two blocks as he was also playing the defensive end of the floor well in that all-around performance.

While the Charlotte Bobcats were still far from the goal that they envisioned when they drafted Kemba

Walker, one bright spot they could get out of the hole they were in was that both their best player and their young rookie Michael Kidd-Gilchrist were chosen to take part in the Rising Stars Challenge during the All-Star break. Walker had eight points in that game.

Kemba Walker rode the high of participating during the All-Star Weekend and seeing the best superstars enjoying themselves by going for his best four-game run as far as scoring was concerned. Right after the break, he went for four consecutive games of scoring at least 24 points. Walker started by scoring in that number in a win against the Orlando Magic on February 19. He then had 24 again in Detroit before going for 27 versus Chicago and finished up with 24 against the Denver Nuggets. All three of those games were losses, though Walker averaged 24.8 points, 3.8 rebounds, and four assists during that run.

On March 4, Kemba Walker had his third double-double of the season. He finished that loss to the

Portland Trailblazers with 15 points and 11 assists. Though he may have had a good game on the playmaking side of the court, he shot a dreadful five out of 20 in that matchup against Rookie of the Year favorite Damian Lillard. Lillard had 20 points that night.

Another one of Kemba Walker's highlight performances that season was when he went for 29 points on 11 out of 25 shooting in a loss to the Washington Wizards on March 9. He also added six assists and four steals in that performance and matchup against John Wall, another young and talented point guard that ushered in the NBA's future.

Arguably Kemba Walker's best performance that season was on March 27. In that game against the Orlando Magic, he made 13 of his 23 attempts from the field and six of his nine free throws. He had an incredible stat line of 34 points, seven rebounds, nine assists, two steals, and two blocks. More importantly, he led the way to a victory for the Bobcats.

Right before the season was about to end, Kemba Walker went for another four-game run of scoring at least 20 points. He started by going for 28 points in a loss to the Detroit Pistons on April 12. Walker then had 21 against the Bucks before going for 23 points and 13 assists versus the Knicks. He ended the regular season with 24 points and seven assists against the Cleveland Cavaliers in a matchup against Kyrie Irving. The Bobcats won all three of their final games.

At the end of an improved season for him, Kemba Walker averaged 17.7 points, 3.5 rebounds, 5.7 assists, and 2.0 steals. As the established go-to guy and best player in Charlotte, he led his team in scoring, assists, and steals. Despite that, his team was still a disappointing squad, having won only 21 games during the season. Nevertheless, it was a stark improvement from the terrible one the Bobcats had a year before.

## Playoff Debut

Coming into the 2013-14 regular season, Kemba Walker and the Charlotte Bobcats got a boost in the form of Al Jefferson, a bruising and dominant inside presence. The large center's presence provided what the Bobcats had lacked for several years already. They finally had a player that could put pressure on interior defenders by being dominant inside the paint and on the post.

The addition of a player he could dish the ball inside during one of the slashes to the basket meant that Kemba Walker's life would be a lot easier and that he would not have to worry about getting much of the defense's attention. This also gave the Bobcats the option of giving the rock to Jefferson inside the paint. The veteran big man became the team's top option on offense while the selfless Walker continued to lead the team at the point.

While Kemba Walker and the Bobcats may have dropped their opener that season, the third-year point guard made up for it by going for 23 points in a win over the Cleveland Cavaliers on November 1 in their second game of the season. Four days later, Walker led the way to the team's second win by going for 25 points on nine out of 20 shooting from the field against the New York Knicks in front of the very people he used to play with when he was a teenager.

However, early on during the regular season, Kemba Walker found himself in an inconsistent slump. There were nights when he went for good scoring nights but went for an awful shooting day in another outing. In his first 12 games of the season, there were three occasions on which Walker was dreadful from the field. He had five points on a two out of 13 shooting night on November 6 in a win against the Toronto

Raptors. A week later, he made his only field goal as against 13 attempts when the team won in Boston. In a loss to Chicago on November 18, he made only three of his 14 shots. Despite such inconsistencies, Walker and the Bobcats had a strong 6-6 record through those first 12 games.

On November 20, Kemba Walker made up for that poor shooting night in Chicago by going for a season-high of 31 points. He shot 12 out of 20 from the field and four out of seven from the three-point line in that game. That game marked a snap of his inconsistencies, and Walker went on to score in double digits for 22 consecutive games.

Walker had excellent performances in that 22-game span. He had his first double-double of the season on December 6 after registering 18 points and ten assists in a win against the Philadelphia 76ers. Three days later, he went on to tie his season-high of 31 points against the Golden State Warriors by making ten of his

18 attempts from the field. What was impressive about that game was that he was as clutch as he has ever been by scoring 27 points in the second half alone. He was responsible for the team's final 15 points of that game.

Then, on December 18, he showed his quality as a clutch performer again. After the Bobcats had been able to go into an extra period against the Toronto Raptors, Kemba Walker had the ball in the final seconds of overtime. When the clock was ticking down, he pulled up for a jump shot over the much bigger Jonas Valanciunas to seal the win for his team at the buzzer. He totaled for 29 points in that game.

It did not take long for Kemba Walker to top his season-high. In a win over the Detroit Pistons on December 20, the third-year point guard had an efficient night of 12 out of 17 shooting from the field to go for a total of 34 points. He also added seven rebounds while making all nine of his attempts from the free-throw line in that game. Then, three days later, he nearly had a triple-double when he went for 25 points, nine rebounds, and ten assists in a win over the Milwaukee Bucks.

Kemba Walker's streak of double-digit scoring ended when he shot two out of ten from the floor to score only six points in a loss to Portland Trailblazers on January 2, 2014. However, Kemba quickly bounced back two days later by going for 30 points on 12 out of 19 shooting from the field and four out of six from the three-point line to give his team a win against the Sacramento Kings. Unfortunately for him, a sprained left ankle he suffered on January 18 left him out of the Bobcats' games for seven consecutive outings.

Upon Kemba Walker's return to action on February 4, the Bobcats won against the Golden State Warriors. However, Walker only shot three out of 11 from the floor for a total of only seven points. It seemed like his injury was still bothering him. The next three games were not easy for him, either. In the four games following his return, he averaged only 12 points and convert only 32% of his shots.

After a long break because of All-Star Weekend, Kemba Walker seemed like he was in full form. He led a win against the Detroit Pistons with 22 points on eight out of 16 shooting. After that, he went on to decimate the very same team on February 19 by going for 24 points and a new career-high of 16 assists. The Bobcats ended up winning that one as well. Walker then capped off a four-game winning run by going for 31 points, eight rebounds, and five assists in a win over the Memphis Grizzlies on February 22.

The apparent problem for Kemba Walker from then until the end of the season was that he was becoming inconsistent. He went for good shooting and scoring one night but fell into a three or four-game slump soon after. Considering such, the point guard played more like his position to make do for what he lacked in consistency. Kemba Walker went for five double-digit assist games in his final 20 games of the season.

He first had 20 points and 14 assists in a win over the Cleveland Cavaliers on March 7. Nearly 20 days later, he went for 20 points and 12 assists against the Brooklyn Nets in another win. Then, on March 31, he had 21 points and ten assists versus the Wizards before going for a triple-double output of 13 points, ten rebounds, and ten assists against the Orlando Magic. He capped it off with 17 points and 12 assists versus Washington on April 9. All of those games were wins. If Walker was not putting up double-digit assist games, he was dishing the ball well, having averaged 7.7 assists from the start of March until the end of the regular season, though he shot 35% from the floor.

After his third season, Kemba Walker averaged 17.7 points, 4.2 rebounds, and a career-best 6.1 assists. However, inconsistency got the better of him, and he shot only 39% from the floor that season. Nevertheless, he was integral in the Charlotte Bobcats' return to the playoffs. The team finished the regular season 43-39.

Kemba Walker's playoff debut was a trial by fire. His team's first-round opponents were the Miami Heat trio of James, Wade, and Bosh. The dominant threesome had just won the last two NBA titles and were once again favorites for a third consecutive one. The Charlotte Bobcats had the odds stacked against them.

Kemba Walker did not go down without a fight. He scored 20 points in his first playoff game against a team that played pretty good defense. The Heat ended up winning Game 1. Game 2 was gritty. The Bobcats kept coming and were not willing to go down easy. Though Walker may have shot a weak clip from the field, he was the gear that ran the machine with Al Jefferson out with an injury throughout that series. He had 16 points that game before scoring only 13 in Game 3. With his back against the wall, Kemba Walker shot 11 out of 15 from the field in Game 4 to score a franchise playoff record of 29 points in what was eventually be another loss to the Heat. Miami ended up sweeping Charlotte with that win in Game 4.

## A Season of Stagnancy

Before the season started, it became official that the Bobcats was now called the Hornets after New Orleans dropped that identity. Coming into the 2014-15 season, the Charlotte Hornets were expected to build on a surprisingly successful previous year that saw them getting to the postseason after several years of missing it. However, it was not the case. Al Jefferson did not get back to the dominant self that he was the previous years. Meanwhile, the young guys were still not ready to step up. It was up to Kemba Walker to bail the team out once more.

Kemba Walker opened the season scoring 26 points on nine out of 26 shooting from the field in a win over the Milwaukee Bucks. He also added six rebounds and five assists in that performance and was the defining player of that night. The Hornets came into the fourth quarter trailing by 24 points until Walker staged the furious rally. He forced overtime with under two seconds to go by draining a three-pointer. After that, he won the game by drilling in a perimeter jumper in overtime. However, after that match, he seemed to start slowly in that season. It took time for him to go over the 20-point mark again.

Despite another scoring and shooting slump for him, Walker managed to get some decent all-around performances early on. He had 15 points, nine rebounds, and ten assists in a win over the Atlanta Hawks on November 7. Two weeks later, he had another near triple-double after registering 15 points, 12 rebounds, and eight assists in a loss to the Orlando Magic. Then, in what was the eighth loss of what was to become a 10-game losing skid, Walker went for 13 points and 13 assists.

Kemba Walker was nothing short of awful in the early stages of the season. For a point guard that averaged nearly 20 points per game the past two seasons, Walker only averaged 14 points on 36% shooting in his first 18 games of the season. His other numbers were not even that impressive. He averaged 4.6 rebounds and 5.7 assists.

The second time that Walker scored over 20 points that season came on December 3 in a loss to the Chicago Bulls. Kemba had 23 points on seven out of 18 shooting that night. Despite breaking the 20-point barrier, he was still shooting a poor clip from the floor. Kemba Walker had seemed to have peaked. Defenses were catching up on him and were learning how to defend him. His jumper could not save him either. However, he made a jumper to win a game against the Knicks the following bout. He only had 11 points that night.

Kemba Walker seemed to have temporarily found his stroke and scoring touch when he went for a then-season high of 28 points in a loss to the Memphis Grizzlies on December 12. He shot 11 out of 21 from the field in that game. Three days later, he went for 24 points, five rebounds, and five assists in a loss to the Cavaliers after shooting just three out of 11 in a loss to the Brooklyn Nets a game before.

Soon after that performance, Kemba Walker was slowly getting back to form. He had 27 points in a loss to the Phoenix Suns on December 17 before going for a new season-high two nights later. In that win against the Philadelphia 76ers, Kemba Walker shot 13 out of 23 from the field to go for 30 points. He followed that up with 20 in a win over the Utah Jazz on December 20.

It did not take long for Kemba to go out and put on a scoring show. On December 27, he had a new career-high in points. Walker shot 15 out of 31 from the field, five out of 12 from the three-point line, and seven out of nine from the foul stripe  for a significant output of 42 in a loss to the Orlando Magic. This was one night after he was clamped down to only six points in a loss to the Thunder. Walker's 35 second-half points in that loss to Orlando was also a franchise-best for a half.

The start of January 2015 was probably the best stretch Kemba Walker had that season. He had 30 points on ten out of 21 shooting from the field in a win over the Magic on January 3. Following that game, Walker went for 33 points on 12 out of 26 shooting from the floor when the Hornets won in Boston. He ended a three-game scoring run of putting up at least 30 points with 31 points on 12 out of 24 shooting from the field in a win over the New Orleans Pelicans on January 7. It was also during that game when he drilled his third game-winner that season. With those three consecutive performances, Walker became only the fourth player in franchise history to put up at least 30 points in three successive games.

Kemba Walker was not done. He went for 29 points on January 8 when he made 12 of his 25 shots in a win against the Toronto Raptors. He followed it up with 28 points against the New York Knicks in a blowout victory before going for 28 again in a loss to the San Antonio Spurs. The Hornets opened January with a 5-2 record. In that seven-game span, Walker averaged 27 points, 4.7 rebounds, and 4.6 assists while shooting 45% from the field.

Just when Kemba Walker had found his shooting stroke and groove, bad luck quickly came his way. Walker got sidelined for a span of about six weeks following surgery to repair a torn lateral meniscus in his left knee. The Hornets missed his presence and instead relied on veteran scoring point guard Mo Williams during his absence.

Kemba Walker made his return on March 11 after six weeks of absence. However, he was still trying to get back to his near All-Star form. He played only 16 minutes off the bench to score six points in a loss to the Sacramento Kings. Following that loss, the Hornets won against the Bulls two days later when Kemba scored ten points in his 28 minutes of play.

On March 20, Walker made his first start since returning from injury. He had 18 points on a poor shooting night in a loss to the Kings. Walker then had 16 points two days later in a win against the Minnesota Timberwolves. Walker then scored over 20 points for the first time in more than six weeks when he had 29 on an 11 out of 24 shooting clip in a loss to the Chicago Bulls on March 23.

The next time Kemba Walker scored over 20 points was on March 28. He had 21 points, five rebounds, and six assists that night. The Hornets ended up winning that one against the Atlanta Hawks. Walker then followed up with 28 points and 12 assists when Charlotte lost to the Boston Celtics in the final game of March. Walker shot nine out of 20 from the field in that match. The last time he scored at least 20 was on April 4. He had 24 points on 11 out of 21 shooting in a win against the Sixers.

In 62 games in what was an injury-riddled and stagnant season for Kemba Walker and the Charlotte Hornets, the point guard averaged identical numbers to what he was averaging the past three seasons. He had 17.3 points, 3.5 rebounds, and 5.1 assists. His percentage from the floor did not improve, either. He was shooting under 39% that season. Charlotte missed the postseason that year.

While Kemba Walker was a capable point guard in his right, especially when he had it going, the problem was that he was mostly inconsistent. There were nights when he exploded for some of the best scoring performances you can get out of a point guard. Those nights were few in between poor performance where he shot below 40% or even 30% from the floor.

What was suspected to be Kemba Walker's problem was his shooting stroke. Walker had been almost exclusively a slasher and attacker all his life. He was already a complete point guard as far as attacking the basket was concerned. He got rid of defenders with slick crossovers. He got them off-balanced with pump fakes. He could blow by his man off the dribble and was never afraid to get the contact at the rim.

Kemba's jumper was only a secondary weapon for him. However, such a weapon was not reliable. There were games when he drained them in bunches, but those nights were rare. When the driving lane was taken from him, Walker struggled shooting the jump shot. He did not command any respect from the perimeter or beyond the three-point line, where he had shot 32% since his rookie season. If Walker wanted to get to the next level, fixing his shot was the first thing he had to do.

# The Rise of Kemba Walker

The suspected problem in Kemba Walker's game was always his jump shot. As statistics showed, among the 210 players that made 100 jump shots the entire season, Kemba ranked 178th when it came to effective field goal percentage on those jumpers.[vi] For a player looking to be an All-Star, that number was not very delightful to take in.

Though there were obvious problems in Walker's ability to hit the jump shot, some may even look at the roster and blame it as to why the point guard was struggling. Nobody was a consistent three-point threat on that team. Outside of Mo Williams, none of the other players were able to convert more than two three-pointers per game. Even Gary Neal, who used to be one of the best shooters when he was with the Spurs, struggled to make his three-pointers.

The lack of consistent shooters on the team meant that Kemba Walker was having trouble with spacing.

Defenses were packed. Every other defender sagged off their man just to get to Walker quick enough for the help defense. Even though the Hornets were having troubles with spacing the floor, Walker was having problems himself as far as getting a consistent jumper up in the air was concerned.

Kemba Walker knew this. He was aware that defenses were sagging off him to take away his drives. During pick and roll situations, his man went under the screen to prevent him from losing the defender. Kemba Walker wanted defenders to be more honest with him. While Walker had a good mid-range jumper, defenses knew his weaknesses from beyond 20 feet or so. Kemba intended defenders to stay home on him during screens. He could blow past them when they tried to fight off the screener. If they wanted to go under the screen, he could drain the three-pointers that nobody expected him to make.[vi]

There was already a vision in the mind of Kemba Walker. He saw himself being able to hit three-pointers off the dribble during pick and roll situations. He saw himself pulling up from a distance or the perimeter whenever his man defended his drive. The only thing left was to plan it all out and make sure the vision came true.

The Charlotte Hornets hired Bruce Kreutzer as an assistant to help the players improve their shooting. He asked Kemba Walker to shoot jumpers alone in an empty gym and had the whole process filmed. Though he saw that Walker's form did not need a complete makeover, Kreutzer broke down the fundamental problems as to why the point guard was struggling with his shot.

Kreutzer said that shooting started from the ground up. The fundamentals of shooting the ball are not predicated on release alone but also on how a player uses his feet. He saw that Kemba Walker's footwork was the underlying problem. It was a problem with which most guards struggled. Walker was jumping off his heel and drifted and faded backward on most of his shots. While the other parts of Walker's jumper were already fine, Kreutzer also noticed that he was shooting the ball in front of his face. This led to a disrupted vision of the basket.[vi]

Repetition was vital the entire offseason for both Kemba Walker and Bruce Kreutzer. The shooting coach asked the point guard to re-align his feet to have him jumping off the balls of his feet instead of his heels. This allowed his body to stay square to the basket during the initial lift. He also trained Walker to adjust his shooting form so that he could shoot and release the ball a little to the right of his face instead of directly in front of it.[vi]

The fixed form also allowed Kemba Walker to shoot the ball quicker than he ever did. In his old shooting form, Walker was drawing the ball from his left hip, traveling it across his body and in front of his face for the pull-up shot. While there were not many problems with that form, there was a slight delay in the release. This allowed defenders to recover and contest his shot. When Kreutzer trained Walker to shoot the ball from the right side of his body, he needed less time to get to his shooting motion. It was a form that fit the alignment of his body.[vi] The only thing left for Kemba Walker to do was to use what he learned during the offseason.

However, things did not come easy for Kemba Walker. He used his new shooting form during the preseason and still struggled with his three-point shooting. He thought that what he was doing was not enough and that his offseason shooting drills did not work. He wanted to go back to his old shooting form. Feeling like he was not in the best position to tell Walker otherwise, Kreutzer told the point guard to consult his head coach first.

Head coach Steve Clifford heard what Kemba Walker had to say. He did not tell him to stick with his new shooting form, nor did he stop him from reverting to his old release. Instead, he told Walker that he could go back to his previous shooting form and shoot in the low 30s and stay as a mediocre NBA point guard. His coach's words got stuck into his head. He went on to stick to his new shooting form, hoping that things would change for him.

Still trying hard to get rid of old habits, Kemba Walker initially struggled to adjust to his new shooting form at the start of the season. During his first five games, he only averaged 15.2 points on a 38% shooting clip. It would seem as though he did not put much effort in the offseason to improve himself.

Kemba Walker broke out by putting up 27 points on a shooting clip of 11 out of 15 from the field in a blowout loss to the San Antonio Spurs on November 7, 2016. The point guard again saw a tough stretch shooting 30% from the floor over the next four games, where he averaged merely 11.5 points. Old habits die hard, and Kemba Walker had to practice what he learned during the offseason to prevent any relapses.

The first time Kemba Walker scored over 30 points that season was when he put up 31 markers on 12 out of 21 shooting from the field in a loss to the New York Knicks on November 17. From then on, everything seemed to improve for Walker. He was beginning to shoot a lot better from the floor. He seemed more confident, and the Hornets were doing better. Barely a week later, he went for a new season-high of 39 points. He made 16 of his 23 baskets that game and also shot four out of six from the three-point line in that win against the Sacramento Kings.

Kemba Walker steadily got better and more consistent since then by regularly figuring himself in double-digit scoring with occasional offensive explosions in between. On December 11, he had 33 points on 12 out of 19 shooting from the floor and five out of eight from the three-point area in a win in Memphis. Near the end of the month of December, Walker put up 38 big points, six rebounds, and five assists in a win against the LA Lakers. He made 14 of his 25 baskets in that game.

Walker had a solid first month of 2016. He started January scoring 32 points in a loss to the OKC Thunder on the second day of the month. He was then consistent throughout the month while trying to get himself and his Charlotte Hornets out of a deep hole. They ended up losing seven consecutive games, but Walker broke the skid by going for 23 points in a win over the Atlanta Hawks on January 13.

Pretty soon after that, Kemba Walker broke records. In an overtime win against the Utah Jazz on January 18, the much-improved point guard nearly had a triple-double on top of a new career and franchise record in scoring. Walker hit 16 of his 33 baskets from the floor, six of his 11 three-point attempts, and 14 of his 15 foul stripe shots for a total of 52 points. He also added nine rebounds and eight assists to nearly become one of the few players in NBA history to record a 50-point triple-double. The previous record set by a Hornets player was 48 points by Glen Rice nearly two decades back.

Two days after that record-breaking performance, Kemba Walker scored 21 in a loss to OKC before going for another high-scoring performance on January 22. In that win in Orlando, Kemba finished the game with 40 points, seven rebounds, nine assists, and four steals. He shot 14 out of 28 from the floor and ten out of 12 from the free-throw line. He then combined for 50 points over the next two games though he was shooting pretty poorly in those wins against the Knicks and the Kings. In the last five games including that 52-point performance, Walker averaged 32.6 points, 5.6 rebounds, and 6.4 assists despite shooting only about 40% from the field. The Hornets only lost one of those five games.

While Kemba Walker did not explode for high-scoring outputs anytime soon, he showed the type of consistency reserved only for some of the best scorers in the league. In all the eight games he played in February save for one night, he scored above 20 points, though he was not considered an All-Star. The man snubbed from the mid-season classic went on to average 24.1 points, 4.6 rebounds, and 5.6 assists in that span. He also shot 46% from the floor in those eight games.

Kemba then started the first five games of March like a house on fire. He averaged 31.6 points, 5.8 rebounds, and 6.8 assists in those first five outings. What was more impressive was the 53.3% shooting clip he had. All five games were wins. Walker then led the Hornets to two more wins to record seven consecutive victories for his team. He averaged 28.6 points, five rebounds, and 6.9 assists in that seven-game winning streak. He scored at least 30 points four consecutive times during that run.

After that seven-game streak ended, Walker willed his team to a good playoff position by leading the Charlotte Hornets to win 11 of their final 17 regular-season games. In that span, Walker averaged 18.8 points, 4.4 rebounds, and 4.9 assists. He nearly had a triple-double in one of those games, which was a win in Philly. He had 27 points, nine rebounds, and 11 assists in that outing.

At the end of the season, Kemba Walker found himself averaging a career-best of 20.9 points. He also added 4.4 rebounds and 5.2 assists. Walker's field goal percentage increased to 42.7%. What impressed the rest of the league was how much improved he was as a shooter from deep. After attempting only 4.5 shots from the three-point area the previous season, he increased the number to six attempts per night that season. Despite that, his shooting clip from deep only increased. He averaged 37% from the three-point area after four years of suffering poor shooting percentages from that distance. The work in the offseason paid off, and it was time to take what he had learned to the postseason. The sixth-seeded Hornets won 48 games during the 82-game regular season.

The Charlotte Hornets entered the playoffs riding high with confidence against a third-seeded Miami Heat team. However, the Heat immediately battered them in Game 1 taking it by 32 points. Kemba only had 19 in that match. However, Walker performed better in Game 2 by tying his career-high and the franchise's playoff high in points. He had 29 on 12 out of 29 shooting in Game 2. However, the Hornets did not play as well as he did. Charlotte ended up losing that game as well.

Game 3, however, was a different story. Kemba Walker tapped into his 2011 NCAA Tournament self and will his team to victory despite another terrible shooting night. He only had 17 points on four out of 19 shooting, but the rest of the Hornets stepped up big. In Game 4, it was all Kemba Walker after registering a new career and franchise high for points in the playoffs. He shot 13 out of 28 from the floor to record 34 total points in another victory for the Hornets. While he was brought down to earth with a poor shooting night in Game 5, the Charlotte Hornets won three consecutive games to take the series lead.

Up three games to two, Kemba Walker and his Hornets seemed to be in great shape heading home to Charlotte to close the series out and win their very first playoff series in a long time. Walker got into his clutch mode by basically becoming a one-man wrecking crew again. He shot 14 out of 30 from the field and four out of eight from the three-point line to go for another career and franchise-best in points. Kemba finished the game with 37. However, Miami won that night to force Game 7.

The Heat eventually blew the Hornets out in Game 7 to proceed to the second round. Kemba Walker only had nine points in that critical outing after squandering away their only chance of advancing to the second round. He averaged 22.7 points, three rebounds, and four assists in the seven games he played the entire postseason.

Despite the early exit by the Charlotte Hornets, there were numerous positives they could take from that season. First, the team had finally found its identity. New pickup Nicolas Batum provided excellent production all-around. Young centers Cody Zeller and Frank Kaminski looked promising as Al Jefferson was declining rapidly. Meanwhile, the veterans Marvin Williams and Spencer Hawes were contributing effectively.

However, the biggest positive they could take from that season was, of course, the rise of Kemba Walker. Walker had been stagnant since his rookie year until his fourth season in the league. His statistics were the same. He was a chucker and an inefficient scorer that relied mainly on the volume of shots he took to get to his scoring averages. Meanwhile, the Charlotte Hornets were just as stagnant and inconsistent as he was during those seasons.

By the 2015-16 season, Walker put in all the hard work during the past offseason to transform himself into a complete offensive player. He worked on his shot to become a dangerous shooter from the outside. Defenses had to adjust their strategy to counter the much-improved Kemba Walker. With their leader and best player showing improvements that should have been long overdue, the Charlotte Hornets became one of the better teams in the East after years of feeding wins to the historically better franchises. The Hornets were flying high as Walker could take them.

## First All-Star Season

Despite showing plenty of improvements to his game the past season to rise and become one of the best point guards in the league, Kemba Walker was still often overlooked. He was not selected to take part in the 2016 NBA All-Star Game, not because he was not good enough, but because other guards were playing better than he was. To reach the level of the elites, he had to perform better than Kyle Lowry, John Wall, Isaiah Thomas, and Kyrie Irving.

With the way Kemba Walker opened the season, it looked as if he was trying to outplay every other point guard in the entire league, not only in the East. Through his first five games of the season, Walker scored above 20 points in all but his season debut. He averaged 24.4 points on 47% shooting in those five outings. That included his then-season high of 30 points on 11 out of 22 shooting scored against the Brooklyn Nets on November 4, 2011.

Kemba then went for his first double-double early in the season when the Hornets blew the Indiana Pacers out on November 7. He finished the game with 24 points and ten assists. Two days later, he went for 21 points, five rebounds, six assists, and four steals to give the Hornets a 6-1 record early in the season. Shortly after that, he went on to duel and outplay Toronto's Kyle Lowry. Walker nearly had a triple-double after registering 40 points, ten rebounds, and seven assists. He shot 12 out of 19 from the floor and made seven of his 12 three-point attempts. Lowry and the Raptors ended up winning that game

All in all, it was an impressive start for Kemba Walker. The often-overlooked point guard went on to average impressive All-Star worthy numbers of 23.8 points, 4.1 rebounds, and 5.1 assists during his first 20 games of the season. The Hornets, who were looking to make another playoff appearance, won half of those 20 games despite a quick start.

Kemba Walker was becoming more consistent as the years went by. He consistently scored in double digits the entire season. On top of that, Walker was contributing well from all angles and all facets of the game. While he did not have an explosive December for the Hornets, he was a constant threat whether in scoring or passing.

Walker had his third and fourth double-doubles of the season in the middle of December. On the 17$^{th}$, he finished a win in Atlanta win 18 points and ten assists. Three days later, he had a near triple-double game after finishing with 28 points, eight rebounds, and ten assists. The Hornets also won that game, which was against the Lakers.

Kemba Walker saved his best of December for the last game of the month. Against a powerhouse Cleveland Cavaliers team, he shot 13 out of 22 from the field and three out of eight from the three-point area to record 37 big points in that loss. That performance marked the 31$^{st}$30-point performance in his career. He now ranks second behind only Glen Rice for most 30-point performances in franchise history.

Kemba Walker quickly opened the gates of January 2017 by going for 34 points on 13 out of 20 shooting in a loss to the Chicago Bulls in his first game of the New Year. He also added nine rebounds and four assists in that match. On January 5, he had another 30-point outing by finishing a loss to the Detroit Pistons with 32 points, seven rebounds, and five assists.

Despite steady and consistent performances from Kemba Walker, the same old problem started to plague the Charlotte Hornets once more. The team got into losing streaks and were merely trading wins with losses. One of the deepest streaks they had was a seven-game losing from late January up to the early parts of February. However, in the middle of all that, they received good news. Kemba Walker was selected as a reserve for the Eastern Conference All-Stars. He became the first player in franchise history to make it to the mid-season classic since Gerald Wallace did it in 2010. Only seven players in Charlotte Hornets basketball history were able to become All-Stars. Walker was one of them.

The theme to Kemba Walker's season was not how he was putting up explosive scoring numbers but how he was climbing steadily to the top of the franchise leadership boards. In the middle of the season, he jumped to the second spot regarding most points scored with the franchise. During the season, he passed both Larry Johnson and Gerald Wallace. He only trailed behind Dell Curry in that department. Walker also became only the second player in franchise history to score 8,000 points with the team. Curry was the first, but it took the legendary player more seasons to reach the mark.

While Walker did not have the best All-Star Game debut, he did come back from the mid-season break with plenty of energy and with a renewed vigor in the hopes that he could bring his team to the playoffs. On February 23, upon returning from the All-Star break, he went for 34 points on 11 out of 19 shooting from the field in a loss to the Detroit Pistons. Three days later, he went for 34 points again when the Hornets lost to the Los Angeles Clippers. Yet, in the very next game, he went for 30 points in a win over the LA Lakers.

Since that 34-point performance against the Clippers, Kemba Walker went for a nine-game streak of scoring at least 20 or more points. During that span, he had three 30-point games and two double-doubles—a 24-point, 12-assist, and 8-rebound performance in a loss to the New Orleans Pelicans and a 21-point and 10-assist game against the Chicago Bulls in a loss. During that streak, Walker averaged 27.3 points, 4.1 rebounds, and 5.8 assists while making 4.4 of his 10.4 three-point attempts.

Just when the season was almost at its end, Kemba Walker tried his best to push the Hornets to a possible playoff appearance. On March 31, he had 31 points and eight assists in a win over the Oklahoma City Thunder. Then, on April 4, he went for 37 points on 13 out of 25 shooting from the field in a loss to the

Washington Wizards. Unfortunately, such performances from the improved point guard could not give his team a playoff berth.

That season, Kemba Walker averaged a career-best 23.2 points including four rebounds and 5.5 assists. His 44.4% shooting clip is also the best he has ever gotten. More impressive is the fact that he shot about 40% from the three-point line despite attempting more shots from deep. That showed how much he has improved over the past seasons. The Charlotte Hornets, who only won 36 games that season, needed to improve as a whole and could not always rely heavily on their star point guard.

While Kemba Walker missed the playoffs again, there were many positive takeaways from that season for him. With the way he was playing all season long, he had jumped from being merely an underrated point guard to become one of the best scoring playmakers in the league. Walker did so by becoming a better shooter and by taking what the defense was giving him. Whether he was given space to shoot or room to drive to the basket, Walker saw and understood any defensive lapses and hardly settled on shots he could not make.

In the past, defenses had the luxury of giving Walker space out on the perimeter because he was not a consistent three-point shooter and also was not adept at hitting jumpers off the dribble. They could no longer give him such treatment during the 2016-17 season because he was hitting three-pointers when he had enough space. On top of that, he could also drain mid-range shots off one of his fancy crossover moves. Defenses could no longer gamble on his offense as they did not know whether to keep him away from the basket or to take away his perimeter shooting.

## Second All-Star Appearance

During the 2017-18 season, Kemba Walker proved that his fantastic All-Star season a year ago was not a fluke and was not a product of him being the only source of offense for the Charlotte Hornets. He started the season with 24 points in a loss to the Detroit Pistons on October 18, 2017. His first breakout performance that season was on October 29 when he put up 34 points and ten assists against the Orlando Magic in a win for the Hornets.

In a win over the Milwaukee Bucks on November 1, Kemba Walker hit eight of his 12 shots to go for 26 points. That performance gave him the 193$^{rd}$ 20-point game of his career. As such, he could move past Charlotte Hornets legend Larry Johnson for the franchise record of most 20-point games. He was slowly and steadily climbing the franchise leaderboard and was already making a solid claim as the Hornets' greatest individual player.

On November 10, Kemba Walker had his second double-double performance that season when he went for 20 points and 11 assists in a narrow loss to the

Boston Celtics. A week after that, he put on a fantastic scoring performance in a narrow loss to the Chicago Bulls, who had no answers for the rising All-Star point guard. In that game, Kemba Walker hit 17 of his 27 shots and made five of his nine three-point shot attempts to end up scoring a season-high of 47 points.

After consistently putting up high-scoring marks, Kemba Walker eventually made franchise history on December 4 in a win over the Orlando Magic. In that game, Walker posted 29 points to go along with seven assists to become the only player in Charlotte Hornets history with 200 games of 20 points or more. He was already the greatest and most consistent scorer in the history of the franchise.

While he eventually slowed down a bit as the season progressed, Kemba Walker had a good scoring outburst on December 22 in a loss to the Milwaukee Bucks. In that game, the All-Star point guard hit 13 of his 21 shots to score a total of 32 points. Right before a momentous 2017 ended for him, Walker went on to post 30 points in his last game of the calendar year. It was in a loss to the Los Angeles Clippers on December 31.

Kemba Walker only got better when the new year started. On January 10, 2019, the Charlotte Hornets star went for 41 big points after making 16 of his 28 shots from the field in a loss to the Dallas Mavericks. After that scoring explosion, he continued to perform consistently during the month of January, where he averaged 25.8 points on 43.1% shooting from the three-point area. He ended that month with 38 points while making nine of his 13 three-pointers in a win over the Atlanta Hawks. That three-point shooting record was a franchise record for the Hornets.

January was also a historic month for Kemba Walker. It was during then when he broke the 9,000 mark for career points to become the only other player in franchise history to reach 9,000 points for the

Charlotte Hornets. He also became the only other player aside from Dell Curry to hit 900 career three-pointers after he reached that mark on January 24 in a loss to the New Orleans Pelicans.

The very next game after he scored 38 points, Walker went for his second 40-point performance that season. He hit 11 of his 22 shots and all 14 of his free throws to go for 41 points in a win over the Indiana Pacers. Just six days later on February 8, Kemba Walker went for 40 points in a loss to the Portland Trailblazers. Performances such as those made him deserving of a second consecutive NBA All-Star Game appearance. He was drafted by Team LeBron and tallied 11 points for the winning All-Star squad.

Right after the All-Star Game, Kemba Walker went into overdrive yet again in the hopes of giving his team a shot at the final Eastern Conference playoff spot. On February 22, he went for 31 points in a win over the Brooklyn Nets. Then, just five days later, he went on to have 31 points again after making 11 of his 19 shots and six of his ten three-pointers in a win over the Chicago Bulls. It did not take too long for him to go for 31 again. On March 2, he went for 31 points in a loss to the Philadelphia 76ers.

On March 22, an inspired Charlotte Hornets went on to destroy the Memphis Grizzlies for what was the sixth-highest scoring differential in league history. Of course, Kemba Walker was the one responsible for doing the bulk of that damage. The crafty point guard destroyed his own record and hit ten out of 14 from the three-point line in what was a career night for him from the perimeter. Out of the 13 shots he made, ten were three-pointers. He went on to finish that game with 46 big points. What was most impressive was that he helped his team win by a total of 61 points. As such, Walker only needed to play 28 minutes that night. Had he played longer, he would have surely destroyed his own career record and might have gone on to hit the most three-pointers in a single game.

As amazing as Kemba Walker was that season, the Charlotte Hornets were anything but consistent. They ended up losing five of their final seven regular-season games. As such, they ended up missing the playoffs for a second consecutive season. They ended at the tenth spot of the Eastern Conference with a record similar to last season. As a last hurrah for what was yet another disappointing season for his team, Kemba Walker finally solidified his claim at the top of the franchise. On March 28, he scored 21 points to surpass Dell Curry as the franchise's all-time leading scorer.

At the end of another All-Star campaign for him, Kemba Walker retained his status as one of the most electrifying point guards in the East. The crafty scoring point guard averaged 22.1 points, 3.1 rebounds, and 5.6 assists while shooting 43.1% from the floor. The Charlotte Hornets' all-time leading scorer may have been nothing short of fantastic, but his team still needed to give him help if they wanted to take the next level.

## Elite Status, Final Season in Charlotte

The 2018-19 season was eventually going to be the best one yet for Kemba Walker, who had gone through the worst types of seasons and the most disheartening circumstances to reach the heights he has achieved at that point in his career. Hard work was everything that put Kemba Walker into position, and it was what was responsible for letting him feel like he belonged in the NBA alongside the best players in the entire world.

Flashback to the 2011-12 season, Kemba Walker was a part of that Charlotte Bobcats team that only won seven games in an entire season—arguably the worst in the history of the NBA. In that dreadful rookie season for Kemba Walker, he felt like he did not belong in the league having shot only 36.6% from the floor and was unable to do the things he did back when he was still with the UConn Huskies.

Even before the 2011-12 season, Kemba Walker already felt like he should not have been in the NBA.

At 6'1", he came into the league shorter than most point guards in a day and age where there are so many physically imposing playmakers in the league. During one of his pre-draft shootarounds, Kemba Walker struggled to shoot from the three-point line and thought that the NBA line was "too far" for him.[vii] All he had was his ability to get to the basket using his superior speed and dribbling skills.

As his NBA career progressed, he found out that he could also no longer drive to the basket as often as he did in the past. Defenders took his slashing ability away by clogging the lane and giving him space out on the perimeter. On top of that, NBA defenders are bigger, faster, and much more physical than the ones he faced in college. He found that his small frame was not enough to allow him to get to the basket at will. Walker could not become the offensive threat that he was during his stay at UConn.

From 2015 to 2018, Kemba Walker massively improved as a scorer and could keep defenses honest. He suddenly became a solid three-point shooter after toiling in the low 30s in terms of shooting percentages from the three-point line during his first four seasons in the NBA. In the previous three seasons, he suddenly became a consistent 20-point scorer and eventually a two-time All-Star from 2017 to 2018. How did it get to that point?

The offseason of 2015 was the major turning point in Kemba Walker's career. After spending his first four seasons as a stagnant offensive player that showed little to no growth as a scorer, Walker learned to develop a work ethic that was difficult to match. He became the Charlotte Hornets' best practice player and was sacrificing more and working harder than any of the guys on the roster.[vii]

Walker's hard work first started by learning how to play the pick-and-roll better and knowing what to do during such situations and when it was the best time to make his moves during a pick play. He began showing signs of improvement as a pick-and-roll player as he steadily learned how to take away his disadvantage as a smaller player and turned it into an advantage, especially when trying to drive past bigger defenders. However, even that was not enough for him.

As documented many times over, Kemba Walker needed to learn how to shoot the ball all over again. He had to retool his jump shot and his shooting form so that he could become a better shooter. Walker shifted his release point to the right and began shooting from his toes and leaned forward a bit to shoot the ball faster and faster. According to his shooting coach, doing so allowed him to shoot the ball quicker so that he could avoid getting blocked and so that he could make use of the limited space and time he was given to get his shot off.

His work ethic paid off. Kemba Walker became a very consistent outside shooter for the Charlotte Hornets. His three-point shooting numbers shot up, and he was making and taking more shots from the outside. His improved outside efficiency opened up the rest of his game. Kemba Walker began driving better than he did in the past and was making and taking shots from all angles no matter what kind of look he was getting.

Kemba Walker did not only improve as a shooter. Knowing that he was going to get a lot more driving opportunities because of his improved shooting, he also learned how to finish near the basket better. His size was always a disadvantage, but Walker learned how to make layups and difficult finishes fitting for a person of his height. He began to look a lot like Stephen Curry as he used his natural shiftiness to his advantage and began hitting floaters off big men after getting them off-balanced.[vii] He also learned how to make use of the glass more when going for layups. Everything opened up for Kemba Walker all because he had enough work ethic to change his approach and his shooting.

When Kemba Walker made the All-Star team for the first time back in 2017, he remembered how he saw his wife crying hard in sheer joy after seeing how far her husband has gone with all the hard work he put himself through. Seeing his wife crying at his success did not stop Kemba Walker from working hard. It was only just the beginning for the All-Star point guard.

Kemba Walker still worked hard every night and was the reason why the staff at their practice facility needed to work overtime. When all the lights were turned off, and everyone on the team has gone home, Walker was there in the gym keeping some of the lights on for himself all while making sure he stays true to his new shooting form. He was always wary of the way he shot the ball and how his toes are positioned. It was truly one of the most dramatic evolutions in league history.

Long before Kemba Walker's time in the NBA, Jason Kidd was the model point guard that learned how to shoot the ball. Back in the 90s, an early joke about Jason Kidd was that it was more appropriate to call him "Ason" because he had no "J". Kidd did indeed have a dreadful jump shot early in his career. However, he soon developed into one of the best shooting point guards of his generation and eventually reached 1,988 career three-pointers, which is still 10th all-time in the NBA right now.

Kemba Walker evolved into a better model for point guards who learned how to shoot. While Jason Kidd developed into a respectable three-point shooter that could hit open shots, Walker turned into a deadly outside shooter that only needed a few inches of space to make a shoot whether off a catch or the dribble. He began to earn the same kind of respect that shooters such as Stephen Curry and Damian Lillard commanded from opposing defenses because of his ability to make three-pointers at a high level.

As the NBA transitioned into a league that now puts more emphasis on the outside shot while giving more advantages to shooters ever since Kawhi Leonard got injured back in the 2017 playoffs, Kemba Walker was only going to be a better player and outside threat for the Charlotte Hornets during the 2018-19 season. That season also turned out to be his major break as an elite star in the NBA.

Kemba Walker started the new season with a 41-point outburst in a loss to the Milwaukee Bucks on the Charlotte Hornets' opening game on October 17, 2018. With that performance, Walker owned the highest scoring output of any Hornets player on opening night.

Kemba Walker only continued to tear defenses up to shreds during the early portion of the season. In a win over the Miami Heat on October 20, he went for 39 points while making seven out of 15 of his three-pointers. A week later, Walker went for 37 points in a loss to the Philadelphia 76ers. Overall, he ended up averaging 31.7 points while making 4.6 of the 11.3 three-pointers he was attempting a game during his first seven games that season.

On November 17, all of Kemba Walker's hard work culminated into the finest game he has ever played as a professional basketball player. Against the Philadelphia 76ers, he made 21 of his 34 field goals and all 12 of his free throws to score a total of 60 points. It was a new career-high for him as well as a new franchise-high for the Charlotte Hornets, who have never seen a finer scorer than Kemba Walker.

However, Walker was not in a celebratory mood after that 60-point explosion. Instead of asking for the game ball or celebrating after putting up what was then the league's highest-scoring total at that point of the season, the point guard was upset because of how the Hornets ended up losing that game.[vii] That was an indication that Walker was more concerned with winning than he was with individual accomplishments.

Just two days after that explosive performance against the Sixers, Kemba Walker went for another memorable night. Against the Boston Celtics, the All-Star point guard went for 43 points after making 14 of his 25 shots. The most crucial part about that performance was that he got the win. If anyone were to ask Walker which between the two performances he liked better, he would most probably say that it was his 43-point game because his team ended up with the win.

Through his first 20 games of the season, Kemba Walker was an unstoppable scoring machine. He averaged 28 points and 6.6 assists while shooting 45% from the floor and 38.5% from the three-point arc in those first 20 games. The unfortunate thing was that, even with Walker playing at an elite level, the Hornets were only able to win half of those games.

When defenses learned to adjust to Kemba Walker's improved prowess as a scorer and when the law of averages caught up, the point guard slowed down a bit as the season progressed. Nevertheless, he almost had a triple-double on December 12 when he finished with 31 points, eight rebounds, and nine assists in a win over the Detroit Pistons. Then, on December 29, he went for another scoring explosion by going for 47 points on 18 out of 29 shooting from the floor in a loss to the Washington Wizards.

The first time that Kemba Walker scored 30 or more points during 2019 was on January 12, 2019, in a game against the Sacramento Kings. In that loss, he went for 31 points. Two days later, he finished a win over the San Antonio Spurs with 33 points. A few weeks later, Walker was named a starter for the Eastern Conference All-Stars. He, Larry Johnson, and Eddie Jones are the only Charlotte Hornets players to ever start in the All-Star Game. Also, he and Glen Rice are the only two players to represent the city of Charlotte three or more times as All-Stars.

During the early parts of February, Kemba Walker went for five consecutive games of 30 or more points. It started when he had 37 points, six rebounds, and ten assists in a win over the Chicago Bulls on February 2. Walker had 37 points again on February 9 in a win over Atlanta. He wrapped up the run with 34 points against the Indiana Pacers in a loss. During that span of games, he averaged 34 points and seven assists while shooting 5.2 out of 11.8 from the three-point line.

In his first game after the All-Star break, Kemba Walker went for his third double-double for the month of February. He finished that win over the Washington Wizards with 27 points and 11 rebounds. A night later, Walker hung 32 points on the Brooklyn Nets in a loss. He ended a spectacular month of February with 35 points and five steals against the Houston Rockets in a loss.

Against the Houston Rockets on March 11, Walker had a great all-around performance. He finished that loss with 40 points, ten rebounds, and seven assists. He had a similar output on March 23 when he finished a win over the Boston Celtics with 36 points, 11 rebounds, and nine assists. After that game, he put up two more double-double performances. In the third game of that run, he had 38 points, nine rebounds, and 11 assists in a win over the San Antonio Spurs. Walker nearly averaged a triple-double during that three-game run as he finished it with 29.7 points, 9.3 rebounds, and 11 assists.

Trying his best to give the Charlotte Hornets a playoff spot in what was his finest season as an individual, Kemba Walker finished a loss to the Utah Jazz on April 1 with 47 big points. A night later in a win over the New Orleans Pelicans, he had 32 points while making 12 of his 13 free throws. Then, in the final game of the regular season for the Hornets, Walker had 43 points in a loss to the Orlando Magic.

In those final six games, Walker averaged 34.2 points as he desperately tried to give the Hornets the final spot in the playoffs. He was even named Eastern Conference Player of the Week because of such performances. However, they came up short yet again as the Detroit Pistons edged them out with two more wins. As such, another All-Star season from Kemba Walker ended up getting wasted because his team could not give him the help he needed to make the Charlotte Hornets a playoff contender. Walker may have been great all season long, but his team was anything but fantastic. As such, nobody expected that the 43-point game that Walker had in his final game of the regular season was also going to be his final game with the Hornets.

Regardless of how the season ended for Kemba Walker, what was clear was that he had become an elite player especially after averaging 25.6 points, 4.4 rebounds, and 5.9 assists all season long. On top of that, he connected 3.2 of the 8.9 three-pointers he attempted while also finishing the season with 260 made three-pointers to become only the ninth player in league history to make 250 three-point shots in a single season. Walker also became the only other player in franchise history to score 2,000 or more points in a single season. After it all, he was named to the All-NBA Third Team and became eligible for a supermax contract from the Charlotte Hornets.

Getting named to an All-NBA team made Kemba Walker as elite as any player could be in the NBA. He was finally getting the recognition he deserved and had evolved into a complete offensive player from being a one-dimensional point guard when he was a rookie playing for a seven-win Charlotte Hornets team. From a player who thought that the NBA three-pointer was too far, Walker became one of the best players at shooting pull-up three-pointers and was probably behind James Harden and Steph Curry in that regard. Walker is proof of how far one can go so long as hard work is involved in the process.

Hard work only worked on the individual level for Kemba Walker. He may have developed into a good leader and was the one always pushing his teammates to do better during practices. However, the team still lacked talent. Hard work can only do so much, especially if you consider that no one other than Kemba Walker can consistently create shots for the Charlotte Hornets. It was clear that changes needed to be made either on Walker's part or on the side of the Hornets.

## The Move to Boston

After the conclusion of his best season as a professional basketball player, Kemba Walker was someone who could command a lucrative deal with any team during the offseason. Because he made the All-NBA Third team, he was eligible for a supermax contract extension from the Charlotte Hornets. However, the Hornets were not willing to give him more than $170 million because they wanted to avoid the luxury tax.[viii] This prompted Walker to choose another destination for himself.

The Boston Celtics immediately entered the picture as a suitable team for Kemba Walker. The Celtics had just recently lost star point guard Kyrie Irving to the Brooklyn Nets. They needed another point guard to carry the offensive load for the team, and they found one in the form of Kemba Walker, who agreed to sign with them immediately when they showed interest in him.

Believing that he was not going to get paid the supermax in Charlotte and knowing that the team was not going anywhere especially with the pieces that they had, Walker went to the Boston Celtics via a sign-and-trade agreement that sent guard Terry Rozier to the Hornets. Kemba Walker agreed to sign a four-year $141 million maximum contract with the Boston Celtics.

Kemba Walker was essentially Kyrie Irving's replacement in Boston. The two players are so identical in the sense that they are two of the best ball-handlers in the NBA and that they are high-scoring guards that love to look for their own shots off the dribble. However, the difference between them was that Walker was a much more willing three-point shooter than Kyrie Irving, who preferred taking close and mid-range shots. While Irving ended up with more efficient shooting numbers, the one thing to consider was that he was playing for a much more structured team with several offensive threats compared to the Charlotte Hornets, who only relied on Kemba Walker's offensive brilliance.

That said, if Kyrie Irving could fit well with the Celtics' offense, there was no reason why Walker could not. They are so similar in terms of style of play. However, intangibles should also be considered. In the years he spent in Charlotte, Walker was never a threat to the team's chemistry and never thought of himself as someone bigger and better than his teammates and the entire organization. Irving might have a championship under his belt and a better resume overall, but he was a big reason why the Celtics did not click in his final season with the team. Historically, Kemba Walker is also the healthier player as he has only missed a total of five games in the last four seasons.

Regardless of how Walker fit with the Celtics, what was certain was that he was on his way to play for a historically better organization and a team that has been legitimate contenders in the last three seasons. As such, it will not be farfetched to say that Kemba Walker would finally be able to break his three-year playoff drought during the 2019-20 season.

# Chapter 5: Personal Life

Kemba Walker was born and raised as a New Yorker in The Bronx. He spent nearly his entire life in New York before leaving for UConn for college. Kemba's parents are Paul and Andrea Walker. Paul works as a carpenter while Andrea is a caregiver. Kemba Walker has no American heritage, though he was born and raised American. Paul is a native of the island of Antigua while Andrea is Crucian but was raised in Antigua. Kemba also has three other siblings, namely his sister Sharifa and his brothers Keya and Akil.

Not a lot is known about Kemba Walker's private life outside of basketball. The young player has always kept things to himself despite the glitz and glamor of the life of a professional basketball player. Other than basketball, he is known to enjoy dancing. He has performed numerous times at the Apollo Theater. He is also known to enjoy singing as he once released a mixtape of songs he enjoyed.

Kemba Walker immediately broke into the shoe branding scene after college. A stellar collegiate career and a miracle run towards the NCAA title back in 2011 made him a national sensation. This led the shoe company Under Armour to sign him to a multi-year deal when he was but an NBA rookie in 2011. Walker has since switched to the Jordan Brand after his deal with Under Armour expired.

# Chapter 6: Impact on Basketball

Because Kemba Walker is still in the middle parts of what is projected to be a long and prosperous NBA career, the point guard that grew up in New York and developed at UConn is still yet to make any significant impact in the NBA. However, despite that, Walker did indeed influence basketball. The biggest impact he provided to the sport is himself and the journey he took to get to where he is at this point in his career.

Since he was in high school, Kemba Walker was always overlooked. In Rice High School, it took him until his sophomore year to make the varsity team. When he made the cut, he was not even a starter. He was playing behind a point guard that did not make the NBA. At that time, Walker was deemed too small and raw to become Rice's star point guard.

It took until his senior year with Rice for Kemba Walker to inherit the starting point guard position. He waited his turn all that time without complaining or griping. He was taught by his family to be selfless and wait for any blessings that might come his way. That was how he looked at his situation when he was with Rice. The moment he earned that starting spot, he immediately became a star and was one of the top recruits in the country.

When he got to the University of Connecticut, Kemba Walker was not given the starting point guard position though he was one of the best point guards coming out of high school that season. Walker was playing behind AJ Price, who reached the NBA but was a role player at best. Despite playing the role of a backup, Walker was getting starter's minutes in a deep Huskies team. He had a productive rookie season, though he was not yet ready to get to the next level. Walker was still overlooked.

During his sophomore year in college, Walker became the starting point guard and the team's best player. However, still raw and unskilled, Kemba could not take the country by storm, though he was still a productive starting point guard. Walker could not even lead his team to a berth in the NCAA Tournament. With the showing he had in his sophomore season, Kemba Walker was still not ready to make the jump.

It took until his junior year with the Huskies for Walker to get the attention he needed and deserved as a player. He was the lone offensive gun for UConn, and he knew that. He went into the season confident and more polished of an offensive player. Walker was scoring in bunches and even led the nation in scoring at one point. His UConn Huskies were not a favorite in the Big East conference, yet he willed the team to five wins in five games to earn the Conference Championship.

Walker's journey that season did not end at a Conference title. Kemba headed into the NCAA Tournament with all the confidence in the world. He willed his team against tougher competition on the

Huskies' path to an NCAA title. Walker led UConn to six wins in the tournament to cap off an 11-game miracle run that resulted in a Big East title and an NCAA Championship. The run itself made Walker a national sensation. He won the Most Outstanding Player award, and his stock only improved because of his performance and leadership during the tournament.

The often-overlooked point guard headed into the 2011 NBA Draft as the most accomplished player of the class. No matter how successful a college career Walker had, teams were looking elsewhere. He was selected ninth overall when the other eight teams were looking at younger players that were deemed to have more potential. Among point guards, he was drafted behind Kyrie Irving, who did not even play a lot in college due to injury, and Brandon Knight, whom he defeated in the Final Four of the NCAA Tournament. Both Irving and Knight were bigger, younger, and more offensively polished than Walker.

Kemba Walker was drafted ninth overall by an equally overlooked Charlotte Bobcats/Hornets franchise that was never one of the more successful organizations in the league. Before Walker's rise to stardom, only six players in franchise history have ever become All-Stars. It was a perfect fit. The overlooked point guard had a chance to put the Charlotte organization on the NBA map.

It did not take long for Walker to make an impact. In his rookie season, he was playing behind DJ Augustin, who was deemed a role player at best when he moved on from Charlotte. Walker was not even putting up the numbers he was supposed to average. He was shooting poorly from the field in his rookie season. He did not make an All-Rookie Team. Guys drafted after him were given those spots.

When Walker ascended to the starting point guard spot in his second year in the league, he was putting up good numbers. He scored in bunches and was explosive on some nights. However, he was inconsistent. Walker was seen as a volume shooter that needed to put up numerous shots to average 17 points a night. He was inefficient and inconsistent, his jumper was suspect, and he could not shoot long shots to save his or his team's lives. Kemba Walker was an incomplete player that stagnated for several seasons. At that point, people were questioning if he had peaked early or if he could still actually improve.

Kemba Walker proved everyone wrong by putting in solid work over the summer of 2015. He honed his jump shot and fixed his mechanics. He became a dangerous marksman from a distance in his fifth year in the NBA. Kemba Walker became a complete offensive player that averaged over 20 points a night thanks in large part to how he improved his jumper. Again, he was overlooked. Other point guards were playing better than he was, to the point that even Isaiah Thomas, the final pick of 2011 NBA Draft, was chosen ahead of him for an All-Star spot in the East.

Come the 2016-17 season, Kemba Walker only improved much more by building on the already impressive season he had a year before. He became not only an All-Star but an elite point guard in a league full of some of the best players at that position in NBA history. Walker had finally gained the recognition that was long overdue by grabbing the world's attention with his improved play and by making the Hornets playoff contenders. Two seasons later, he became an elite player and an All-NBA team member.

Kemba Walker's long journey to NBA stardom after years of getting overlooked is what has become his impact on basketball. As his father said, Kemba always waited for his turn. He waited for his turn behind more established starting point guards in high school, college, and in the NBA. When he got his turn, he waited and slowly developed into the player he is today.

What the younger generation got out of Kemba Walker's impact is that he was never too impatient or never in a rush to improve. Even with a historically bad franchise, Walker never complained about his role or the team's place in the standings. He always did his job well without getting too impatient or whining that he never got his due. Walker was taught the right way how to be a person. He took that with him to his NBA career. He plays the game the right way, and he looks at his situation with a positive outlook every time. If his attitude and journey are not considered impacts, then who knows what they are?

# Chapter 7: Legacy and Future

The one legacy that Kemba Walker has without a doubt left in basketball was that miracle run he had as a college player at UConn. Nobody expected the Huskies to compete for a title that season because of their roster makeup. Walker had a good year before that season, but he was not projected to become one of the best college players in recent memory. His best help that season were rookies Jeremy Lamb and Shabazz Napier. Outside of those two, the Huskies were a mediocre bunch.

Walker proved everyone wrong by starting the season like a house on fire. He even led the nation in scoring at one point during those early games. He led the Huskies to upset wins over better-seeded teams. Walker made other point guards dance to the beat of his drum whenever he decided to take it upon himself to take over games. Walker was the heart and catalyst to that improbable run towards a Conference title. It was five games in five days, but Walker fought fatigue and doubt to earn his team that title.

He was not done there. He went into the NCAA Tournament with all of the world's confidence. He helped his team beat higher-seeded and more favored teams in his quest for college immortality. Walker was the cog that drove the Huskies' machine. With every beat of his heart and every breath he took, the UConn Huskies followed. Following those five wins in the Big East conference, Kemba Walker led his team to six more wins to grab the NCAA Title by force and to be named the Most Outstanding Player of the tournament.

When you look at it, rarely do you see players of his size that have led an overlooked team towards a national championship. Kemba Walker defied odds to get to that pinnacle. His miracle run towards that title ranks as amongst basketball's greatest moments. That was a moment and legacy that nobody could ever take away from Kemba Walker's life.

In the NBA, Kemba Walker, among many others in the league today, continues the long legacy started by scoring point guards that used to be a rarity in a league that focused more on forwards and big men in the past. Walker is among the new breed of point guards in this new era of NBA basketball. What used to be a position that led and passed has now evolved into a role that scores more than any other player on a roster. Point guards are now considered the most critical position in basketball not because of their ability to orchestrate offenses or to make plays for others but because of how they score the ball.

Today, point guards have become the leaders in scoring. Russell Westbrook, Stephen Curry, James Harden, and Isaiah Thomas, among others, have risen to become the league's best scorers despite playing a position that is used to pass the ball more often than shooting it. Kemba Walker is among such players that create more offense for himself than for others.

Despite playing in a slow-paced offensive system of the Charlotte Hornets in his first eight seasons, Kemba Walker has risen to prominence for being able to provide the scoring punch needed by the team to win games. The team has always struggled with spacing and shooting, but Walker was always come up big for the team whenever they needed him on the offensive end.

While history dictated that point guards should make their teammates look better by making plays for them or by passing the ball often, today's point guards like Kemba Walker make their teammates better by being scorers. Passing may indeed be second nature to today's scoring point guards, but their aggressive mentality has paved the way for other offensive players to free themselves up in open spots.

Like most of today's offensive-minded point guards, Kemba Walker attracts plenty of defensive attention by attacking the basket hard. This opens up scoring opportunities for others. When he is not attacking the basket, he comes off screens and attracts extra defensive attention during pick and roll situations to free teammates up at their sweet spots on the floor. This has become an evolutionary trend in today's basketball. Point guards may be offensive-minded, but such a mentality has made teams better off.

Other than being the main scoring punch and best player on the Charlotte Hornets' roster (and even in the history of the franchise), Kemba Walker has grown to become the team's most iconic player. As far as history dictated it, he has probably become the franchise's best player already. No one could debate that anymore as he has eclipsed all the scoring records in the history of the franchise.

Concerning scoring, Walker has become the Hornets' all-time leading scorer and has 12,009 career points with that team while only needing to play 605 games to do so. Walker is more than 2,000 points ahead of

Curry, who finished his career with 9,830 points for the Hornets. He has also made a total of 1,283 three-pointers for the Charlotte Hornets and has more than eclipsed Dell Curry's record of 929 three-pointers. That said,

While never the best passing point guard, Kemba Walker has also become the franchise's second-best assist man behind only Muggsy Bogues. As such, he has not only become the team's best scorer but has also become the franchise's most complete point guard because of his ability to put points up on the board and make plays for his teammates.

One of the only seven players in franchise history to become an All-Star, Kemba Walker has already solidified his role in Charlotte Hornets franchise lore. Only Larry Johnson, Alonzo Mourning, Glen Rice, Eddie Jones, Baron Davis, and Gerald Wallace have been named All-Stars while playing in a Charlotte uniform. Save for Gerald Wallace, those players have only experienced short stints with the franchise before moving on to other teams. Walker has also become the only other player in franchise history to make it to the All-Star team thrice. Mourning and Johnson have become All-Stars twice with the team. Meanwhile, Rice did it thrice.

All that considered, there is no argument that Walker has become the Hornets' all-time best player. Kemba has already become the best scorers in franchise history and will probably hold on to his lead for a very long time. He has led his team to two playoff appearances already while also making the All-Star team in the process.

Nevertheless, things had to end for Walker and the Hornets as he eventually chose to depart from that team to join the Boston Celtics. He would have had more All-Star appearances for the Hornets and continued to break records had he stayed there. Walker did what he thought was best for his career. After all, the greatest players are always defined by their achievements as winners. Going to Boston was the best way for Kemba Walker to end up as a winner when all is said and done.

Playing for the Boston Celtics means that Kemba Walker has some heavy shoes to fill. After all, the Celtics organization is one of the two greatest franchises in league history and is consistently a contender. The likes of Bob Cousy, KC Jones, Dennis Johnson, Jo Jo White, and Rajon Rondo have all been successful point guards with the Celtics. As such, it is up to Walker to live up to the legacy of those all-time great Celtics guards.

With the way Kemba Walker is playing right now, he is expected to be an All-Star for a very long time even as the Eastern Conference is full of elite point guards that play better or just as well as the New York product is doing so right now. He has a solid chance of staying at the elite level, or he may even take it by force if he improves even more so than he already has. Now that he plays for the Boston Celtics, he also has a good chance of becoming a more efficient scorer or even a proven winner.

While Kemba Walker may have often been overlooked throughout his entire career as a basketball player, the way he has worked on himself and his game while maintaining the proper attitude and outlook on life and the sport has gotten him to places doubters never thought he could reach. Kemba Walker was a winner in college and is steadily becoming one in the NBA. He has the heart of a lion despite his small size. Such a heart means that only the sky is the limit for how much he could accomplish in his NBA career.

# Final Word/About the Author

I was born and raised in Norwalk, Connecticut. Growing up, I could often be found spending many nights watching basketball, soccer, and football matches with my father in the family living room. I love sports and everything that sports can embody. I believe that sports are one of most genuine forms of competition, heart, and determination. I write my works to learn more about influential athletes in the hopes that from my writing, you the reader can walk away inspired to put in an equal if not greater amount of hard work and perseverance to pursue your goals. If you enjoyed *Kemba Walker: The Inspiring Story of One of Basketball's Most Explosive Point Guards,* please leave a review! Also, you can read more of my works on *Roger Federer, Novak Djokovic, Andrew Luck, Rob Gronkowski, Brett Favre, Calvin Johnson, Drew Brees, J.J. Watt, Colin Kaepernick, Aaron Rodgers, Peyton Manning, Tom Brady, Russell Wilson, Michael Jordan, LeBron James, Kyrie Irving, Klay*

*Thompson, Stephen Curry, Kevin Durant, Russell Westbrook, Anthony Davis, Chris Paul, Blake Griffin, Kobe Bryant, Joakim Noah, Scottie Pippen, Carmelo Anthony, Kevin Love, Grant Hill, Tracy McGrady, Vince Carter, Patrick Ewing, Karl Malone, Tony Parker, Allen Iverson, Hakeem Olajuwon, Reggie Miller, Michael Carter-Williams, John Wall, James Harden, Tim Duncan, Steve Nash, Draymond Green, Kawhi Leonard, Dwyane Wade, Ray Allen, Pau Gasol, Dirk Nowitzki, Jimmy Butler, Paul Pierce, Manu Ginobili, Pete Maravich, Larry Bird, Kyle Lowry, Jason Kidd, David Robinson, LaMarcus Aldridge, Derrick Rose, Paul George, Kevin Garnett, Chris Paul, Marc Gasol, Yao Ming, Al Horford, Amar'e Stoudemire, DeMar DeRozan, Isaiah Thomas and Chris Bosh* in the Kindle Store. If you love basketball, check out my website at claytongeoffreys.com to join my exclusive list where I let you know about my latest books and give you lots of goodies.

# Like what you read? Please leave a review!

I write because I love sharing the stories of influential athletes like Kemba Walker with fantastic readers like you. My readers inspire me to write more so please do not hesitate to let me know what you thought by leaving a review! If you love books on life, basketball, or productivity, check out my website at claytongeoffreys.com to join my exclusive list where I let you know about my latest books. Aside from being the first to hear about my latest releases, you can also download a free copy of *33 Life Lessons: Success Principles, Career Advice & Habits of Successful People*. See you there!

Clayton

# References

[i] Wenzelberg, Charles. "Selfless Star Walker is Heart of Huskies". *New York Post*. 31 March 2011. Web.

[ii] Hamilton, Moke. "NBA Sunday: Kemba Walker's Inspiring Journey". *Basketball Insiders*. 18 January 2015. Web.

[iii] Armstrong, Kelly. "First NYC Point Guard to Make NBA All-Star Game Since '03, Kemba Walker Stays True to Roots". *NY Daily News*. 4 February 2017. Web.

[iv]"Kemba Walker". *NBAdraft.net*. Web.

[v] Givony, Jonathan. "NBA Draft Prospect of the Week: Kemba Walker". *Draft Express*. 30 November 2010. Web.

[vi] Mahoney, Rob. "The Craft: Kemba Walker's Jump Shot". *Sports Illustrated*. 6 January 2016. Web.

[vii] Lowe, Zach. "Kemba Walker never saw this superstar turn coming". *ESPN*. 28 November 2018. Web.

[viii] Bonnell, Rick. "Sources: Kemba Walker letting Hornets know he intends to sign with Celtics". *Charlotte Observer*. 29 June 2019. Web.

Made in the USA
Middletown, DE
03 May 2020